In the Shelter of Her Arms

My Journey from Darkness to Light with

SRI MATA AMRITANANDAMAYI DEVI

by
Gretchen Kusuma McGregor

Mata Amritanandamayi Center
San Ramon, CA

IN THE SHELTER OF HER ARMS
My Journey from Darkness to Light with
Sri Mata Amritanandamayi Devi

by Gretchen Kusuma McGregor

ISBN 1-879410-17-6

First Printing, September 2012

Published by:
Mata Amritanandamayi Center
P.O. Box 613
San Ramon, CA 94583-0613 USA
Ph.: (intl) (1) 510-537-9417
Fax: (intl) (1) 510-889-8585
Websites: www.amma.org, www.theammashop.org

Also available at:
Mata Amritanandamayi Mission Trust
Amritapuri P.O., Kollam Dt., Kerala, INDIA 690 525
Phone: (intl) (91) (476) 2897578 / 2896399 / 2896278
Fax: (intl) (91) (476) 2897678
Email: inform@amritapuri.org
Website: www.amritapuri.org

Dedication

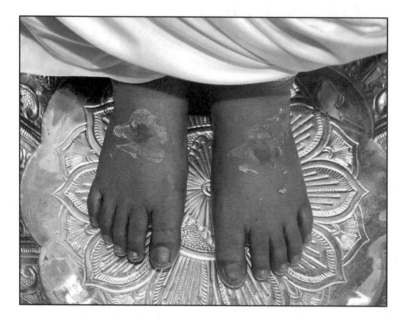

This Book is Humbly Dedicated to

ADI PARA SHAKTI
THE ANCIENT SUPREME DIVINE MOTHER

Who has, in truth,
Incarnated in the form
of

SRI MATA AMRITANANDAMAYI DEVI
The Mother of Sweet Bliss

and to all Her darling children
who have come running

Table of Contents

Prelude

August 1981
Copenhagen, Denmark

Can any of us say precisely when our conscious journey of awakening begins? Oftentimes it is only years later, in retrospect, that we hone in on the exact moment when the first glimmer of Truth caught our eye — when some person or event caused us to become aware of the world as it truly is, and from that moment onwards, never to perceive it as we did before.

For me, it happened in a bookstore near Tivoli Gardens in Denmark. The day was beastly hot for northern Europe, and I had taken refuge in an aisle of books labeled "Mythology," scanning the titles for what might be a good read on the train back to Norway, where I was studying for the summer. The University of Oslo was hosting an eight-week, international summer school for world peace led by the Peace Research Institute of Oslo (PRIO), in which I was enrolled. Little did I know that my weekend getaway to Denmark would change my life forever.

As I was browsing, a book fell off a shelf behind me — literally. Bending down to pick it up and return it to its place, the title caught my eye: *When God Was a Woman* by Merlin Stone. Hmmmmm. Having been raised in a family of devout Protestant agnostics, one of my greatest fears was that someone would one day ask me what I thought about

God. And I would have not a word to say. I was completely ignorant on the subject. So I thought, "Why not?" Being an intellectual, reading a book on a subject that I wanted to be more versed in was a familiar approach. As for God being a woman, now that really tipped the topic on its head. I bought the book.

And read it I did. Or did the book read me? The moment I opened it, I was consumed, unable to put it down until I had read every last page, pored over each footnote, and then started all over again. I was mesmerized as the author recounted a history of the worship of the Great Mother from the most ancient times, touching all corners of the earth. From this survey of the ancient religions of the Divine Mother, a picture of deep compassion and sacred power emerged. The images of the Divine Mother reverberated with a profound truth, the Great Mother as God.

What struck me the most was that such widespread traditions of ancient culture could remain so hidden from modern view. Well-educated and well-travelled, studying environmental science at University of California-Berkeley and participating in the prestigious PRIO summer program, how could this fascinating aspect of human history have been unknown to me? Had I been entirely asleep at the wheel, or just a product of my own culture, which seemed to thrive on the loss of historical memory?

Whatever it was, my heart was on fire with the idea of a Great Mother! If she had been worshiped in times past, where was she now when the world needed her most? From where I stood, the need for peace and justice could never have been greater; living in harmony with nature was the need of the hour. Though I was only 20 years old, it seemed that if humanity were to have even a hope at reaching these lofty ideals, then what could be more helpful than having the wind of the Divine Mother beneath our wings? In that reading, my entire worldview shifted. I had been informed of the Mother as the Source of All, and I decided to pursue Her.

I began praying. I had never prayed in my life. But it immediately felt incredibly natural to call on the Great Mother. I began composing songs, little chants really, to the Mother. I started a "spirit circle" with some of my friends when I returned to UC Berkeley at the end of the summer. We would meet in the redwoods or at the Pacific Coast and sing our songs, twirl in circles like dervishes, then sit quietly in what I would later realize was meditation. We would try to visualize the Great Mother and ask her to guide us. I would cry sometimes, thinking of how much the earth and the people and the animals needed the Great Mother to remember them and help them.

One song I still remember writing was...

Goddess of the world, your story is untold,
about how your power was broken, stolen, mystery unfold!
We are many strong women,
daughters of the earth,
gathering together

we will break the chains that bind us,
that possess us, that control us.
Spirit circle give us power,
Let the mystery unfold, let the mystery unfold...

The connection we all felt to the Great Goddess was palpable, but there was no external reference point that could affirm her presence in the modern world. Everything around us was based on materialism, grooming us to become good consumers, cogs in a wheel, soldiers at war. Ronald Reagan was elected, and compulsory registration, i.e. the draft, was re-instated. The Three Mile Island nuclear power plant had a meltdown. We all graduated and went our separate ways. Off to seek the American Dream, whatever that was.

FARM GIRL
Northern California
June 1982

My next stop was a six-month internship at an organic farm in the northern California town of Covelo. My idea was to get out of the urban atmosphere, which felt toxic and distracting, and to learn about practical living in a rural setting. Tuning into the Great Mother might be much easier if I was living in greater harmony with Mother Nature. Up to that point in my life, except for weekend getaways to the Laurel Mountains with my grandfather in western Pennsylvania where I grew up, I was a city girl through and through. But now I was convinced it was time to break one of the more obvious chains that bound me — my complete ignorance about how the majority of the world lived and toiled. To develop my intuition and be guided by my prayers into the arms of the Divine Mother became my dream. My plan was to do something to make the world a better place.

One of my many duties as an intern on the farm was to fetch the two dairy cows from the outlying pasture in the early morning and to milk them — by hand. I remember sitting on the milking stool with my forearms aching intensely from the rigor of milking out nearly five gallons of milk and thinking alternately, "Please don't kick the bucket over, Daisy," and "Somehow this must be connected to the Great Mother!" I would sit there in the midst of that setting and focus intently on the Divine Mother..."Where are You? Where are You?" over and over again. The idea of the Great Mother became fixed in my mind.

Near the end of my six-month stint as milkmaid, I had no idea of what to do next. My East Coast family had an idea though – get a job! I had run out of time to find the Great Mother and now I would bow my neck to the yoke of the nine-to-five workaday world. But at least I could choose where I wanted to live. The best way to figure that out seemed obvious — do a "vision quest." So I rode my bicycle to the highest hill in the Covelo Valley, a place where the Pomo Indian Tribe had gone in the distant past, to seek communion with Mother Earth.

There it was, Thanksgiving of 1982. Off on a quest for my vision, I was leaving it all in the hands of the Great Mother, right? Well, I sat and sat on that lonely hill; I prayed, cried a bit, hours and hours went by. It had been drizzling most of the day, but now it was pouring down. I was so hungry and the Thanksgiving feast was waiting back at the farmhouse. But I hadn't had my vision yet. How long was this supposed to take, I wondered. Now that I was starving and cold, shouldn't that be a gentle nudge to the Mother to come to my rescue? Night was falling, it was getting dark. Clearing my head one last time, I tried to lightly rest my mind on my need to know, "Where? Where? Where?"

Then it came to me, so completely out of nowhere, as clear as a bell, "Mountains of New Mexico... a wise woman is there." Thank you, thank you, Great Mother! That was enough for me to know what my next step was. I tore back to the farm on my bike by the last light of day.

"You're moving to Mexico? But you don't even speak Spanish!" was my family's reaction to the news.

"*New* Mexico," I reiterated, imagining that would be reassuring to them. And, "No, I don't have a job offer. Yet."

Not reassuring to them. But they knew better than to stand in the way of their headstrong eldest daughter. I arrived in Taos, New Mexico by the New Year.

MOUNTAIN GIRL

January 1983

Taos, New Mexico

I was all of 22 and could feel the magic. I was opening my life up to the Great Mother. The mountains and canyons and the river Rio Grande became my source of inspiration. It was easy to feel the presence of the Divine Mother there; she was just about everywhere. Late afternoon rainbows, sage-scented air where desert cactus bloomed moments after the precious rainfall, the piercing midnight howl of coyotes. As a backdrop to it all, the Sangre de Cristo Mountains, sacred to the Taos Pueblo Tribe, towered up 12,000 feet.

Within a week I found a job as a short-order breakfast cook at the Apple Tree Restaurant. Not exactly what my family had in mind, but a job nonetheless. The first of their five children was supporting herself, and they weren't going to argue with that. For my part, a wee bit over-educated for my job, I felt absolutely certain about the move. I had been guided here and had no choice but to wait patiently.

Throughout the winter my trusty bicycle carried me the two miles to work in the pre-dawn hour; freezing cold air assailing my lungs at an altitude of 7,000 feet, bike tires crunching over the icy roads with neighborhood dogs nipping at my heels to make sure there was no trespassing on their watch. Afternoons found me glade skiing

recklessly down the double black diamonds at the Taos
Ski Valley. And my prayers continued, pouring from my
heart. One oft-repeated chant was:

> *We all come from the Mother,*
> *To Her we shall return*
> *like drops of rain,*
> *flowing to the ocean...*

RIVER GIRL

Summer 1983
Pilar, New Mexico

That summer I took a position as a café cook in Pilar,
a village of 200 inhabitants just south of Taos, now affectionately known as the Pilar Yacht Club Café for its
close proximity to the Rio Grande rafting community.
My idea was that living close to the river would help at-
tune me to the Great Mother. As it turned out, I met a
local family who offered me free lodging in a tiny camper
parked right on the bank of the river. The mother of the
household, such as it was, was named Meadow. She had
two daughters, Ajna and Riversong. Meadow and her
daughters had come to know of my profound attraction
to the Great Mother and had similar leanings. Little did
I know then how great Meadow's gift would be.

Swimming replaced skiing as a daily summer pastime;
I would dive into the brisk snow melt of the Del Norte
headwaters first thing in the morning, just to feel it take

my breath away. To commune with the Great Mother at that moment was practically effortless; to enter a dreamy state sitting cross-legged in the emerald green meadow next to the flowing river was enchanting. Sitting there by the banks of the river, I couldn't help but wonder when I would meet the "wise woman" who had summoned me here and what would happen after we met. Would it take many years for that part of my destiny to unfold? Would my ability to sense the Great Mother guiding me continue? Would I ever find her in this world?

Sitting on the riverbank as the sun was setting, I would call out a well known Goddess chant and sometimes tears would come:

…Isis, Astarte, Diana, Hecate, Demeter, Kali, Inana…

These were the various names of ancient goddesses that I had read about. I chose to remain hopeful that she might hear my call.

BINGO!

August 1983
The Pilar Café

"I just met a man who saw the Divine Mother in India. And he has pictures!" exclaimed Meadow one afternoon. "He just moved to the village. You have to meet him." I will never forget that moment as long as I live. I was standing behind the counter in the café wearing an apron badly stained with red chile sauce over my favorite swimsuit and a mid-length blue jean skirt. My flip-flops were still wet from my lunchtime swim.

Only years later would I realize that her pronouncement was the next pivotal moment in my life. It was one of those moments that 'clicks.' When you know something big just happened, or is about to. It's the smooth feeling of a key fitting into a lock and the door opening. The tuning of a perfect note on the guitar string. The loosing of an arrow as it meets its mark.

Pilar was a small village, and not many days passed before the newcomer happened into the cafe for a bite to eat. I practically leaped over the counter to take his order. Trying to appear nonchalant when returning with his food, I queried, "So, are you the one who met the Divine Mother?" With a sidelong glance and deep baritone voice came his measured reply, "Yes, I am." I could hardly contain my excitement. It must have showed though because he added, "If you're interested, I'm doing a slide show on Saturday." I introduced myself and asked his name. "Greg McFarland," he replied.

KANI DARSHAN: FIRST DARSHAN

Saturday could not have come soon enough, but the evening of the slide show finally arrived. I rode my bike to the small adobe cottage overlooking the river. The sky was memorable that night displaying the full range of summer sunset colors that made Georgia O'Keefe's brushstrokes world-famous. Surprisingly, not a single other person attended the slide show — I was an audience of one. When I saw the first slide of 'Ammachi,' as Greg called her, I sat in stunned silence. The light from her eyes burned away a fog in which I had been unconsciously enveloped my entire life.

The immediacy of Ammachi's presence was undeniable. I mean, there she was, right there in the room with us. I knew then that I had to go and meet her. In silent awe, I watched the rest of the slide show and remember barely a word of what Greg said. When the projector clicked off I blurted, "I'm going there!"

"But you can't just go there," came Greg's reply. "There is nothing there, just Amma's family home and a few huts. It's not possible to simply arrive; you have to write to Amma first."

DEAR AMMA

And so I did. The very next day, on a self-stamped, blue aerogram I wrote:

Dear Amma,

I would like to come and meet you. I think you have the answers to all my questions. Please, may I have permission to visit?

Gretchen

My passport application went out the same day. There was a distinct shift in my life, and I could not put Amma's starry eyes out of my mind. So many times in a day I would think to myself, "Oh, I am on a journey to meet the Divine Mother!"

A chance to take a free raft trip down the mighty Colorado River came my way. Being a short order cook, I was a valuable asset on a three-week, 300-mile escapade through the Grand Canyon. So I thought, "Why not? It will take at least a month for my letter to reach India and for Amma to send a reply. What an opportunity to immerse myself in nature in the meantime."

DOWN THE RIVER

The Colorado River is no joke. It runs about 600,000 cubic feet per second. The earth is shivering with the turbulent power of that volume of water tumbling up against the riverbanks where you put in at Lee's Ferry, Arizona. The New Wave Rafting Company of Santa Fe was hosting the trip for its employees. The raft I would travel in was piloted by Greg McFarland. The whole three weeks I got to hear stories about his visit the year before to meet Amma! One day he told me that Amma had given him a mantra that he could share with anyone he met that seemed like they might be one of Amma's children. I didn't know anything about mantras, but the more he explained about it, the better it sounded. So he wrote down the mantra on a piece of paper and explained how to use it. I devised a way to keep track of my repetitions on my fingers so that sets of 108 could be done.

The effect of that chanting each morning and at various moments throughout the day was different from anything I had experienced before. There was a subtle shift in my mind that made me feel extremely peaceful. I became very receptive to nature, which was all around us. The vibration of the mantra would course through me as the rounds of *japa* (repetition of mantra) went on increasing. I was so happy sitting on that little raft, chanting this new thing called a mantra, and taking in the Grand Canyon's majesty as we floated by. Constant daydreams about meeting Amma soon filled my thoughts.

Returning to Santa Fe from the trip in the middle of October, one of the first things I did was to go to the post office. There was never much there. Peering through the little glass window of my mailbox I felt a thrill when, clearly visible, there was a blue aerogram resting diagonally against a small parcel — my passport!

My heart skipped a beat as I noted the return address and carefully tore open the letter. In a script I had never seen, innocent, little-girl letters meandered across the page. It must be Amma's handwriting! Beneath that was a translation of what was written:

Darling daughter,

When are you coming? You are always welcome here. Amma is waiting to see you. Come quickly, darling daughter.

Kiss, Kiss

I was so excited! I was going to meet Amma!

That evening on the phone with my family back in Pennsylvania, the conversation went something like:

"I'm going to India, Mom."

"You're going to Indiana?"

"No, Mom, India," I replied.

"What on earth for?"

"To meet Amma, an Indian saint…."

"But why do that?"

"Because I feel like I have to go and meet her. Don't worry, I have the ticket money; it won't be any expense for you or Dad."

What could they say? Frankly, I think they were happy to have one "out from under the roof," as the saying goes. They knew me well enough to know that once I set my mind on something, there was no point in trying to dissuade me.

CHAPTER ONE

Beggar in the House of God

We set out in early November. The year was 1983. Greg McFarland wanted to travel back to Amma again and take his 15-year-old daughter, Flora, for Amma's blessing. We landed in Chennai and a day later took the overnight train to Kollam. One bumpy rickshaw ride later deposited us at the Vallikkavu boat jetty, and we were there. Staring across the river at an impenetrable wall of dense green, it finally hit me. Amma was just on the other side of the river. A wave of anticipation washed over me, intermingling with nervousness.

The past two years had been spent calling out to the ancient Goddess who, I believed, must be in the world somewhere. What existed then, must exist now — that was my firm conviction. Was she now just a boat ride away? Why not? Since Copenhagen, I had been guided each step of the way as I had opened my heart up more and more through song and prayer. Was I ready to step in the boat and cross over? What was waiting on the other side? Now I felt really nervous!

As the boatman plied the river with his long pole, my mantra easily found its place on my lips. My breath quickened as we clambered out, dragging our bags onto a tiny, narrow path. Glancing down, something carved on a piece of thick black stone embedded in the mud caught my eye. Stopping to look at it, a shiver went down my spine. A perfect circle about five inches across, with a prominent center dot, a symbol unmistakably familiar to me from many, many dreams. Was it just a coincidence, this ancient symbol of the Mother Goddess? A flush of adrenaline shot through me, boosting my confidence that I was on the right path, and about to meet the 'wise woman' for whom I had been searching.

We proceeded for a few moments before the coconut trees thinned out and opened onto a sandy expanse where a small cluster of people were sitting quietly. Without a doubt, there was Amma! She was shimmering with light even from this distance. As we approached, everyone stood up and Amma stepped forward. She embraced Greg, then Flora. Turning to me, Amma's smile was 1,000 watts. Her eyes were piercing stars. Now I was in Amma's arms, and my heart burst like a dam. The sensation was one of excruciating joy, as if a column of intense happiness, more than could be imagined, was flowing from my feet to the top of my head. I could feel hot tears streaming from my eyes, and Amma sat down, pulling me to rest my head on her lap.

My first ever inner vision formed; a double helix, like a DNA strand, which was iridescent and luminous, awash with soft color. Awareness that Amma was one side of the strand, and I was the other. We were entwined as far into the past as could be seen, and just as far into the infinite future. The point of co-incidence was this very moment of meeting again. That point was emitting a strong pulse of light. In that instant I knew that I had found the Divine Mother in this lifetime. That everything which had happened to me up to this point in my life was only to bring me back to Her. That I had always known Her, would know Her again now, and would always know Her in the future. How much time went by I could not say, but then we were all getting up and Amma's skirt was wet with my tears.

As I got to my feet there was a feeling of floating above the ground. The expression "on cloud nine" came to mind. As if someone had removed a 50-pound rucksack from my back that I didn't know I had been carrying. Later I learned that when we meet our Guru there is a transfer of our karmic burden. The Guru lightens our load. The sensation of that occurring was instantaneous. A young Western woman brought a fresh skirt for Amma and smiled a welcoming smile.

Amma wanted to take us on a tour so off we went. Her laughter was robust, natural and intoxicating. First stop was at the small temple, the Kalari, just behind where Amma had been sitting. The temple doors were closed, and we sat on the front porch. Amma asked my name. "Gretchen," I said. "What?" the person translating asked. "Gretchen." Silence. We passed onto singing. Amma wanted me to sing something. I was hopeless for singing. Perhaps I was blushing because "Rain, Rain, Go

Away" was suggested. So I sang that and the instruction came that I try to hold the notes steady. Tried that, not terribly successful, so on with the tour.

To the left of the Kalari was a simple rectangular thatched hut with three doors. We went there. The first door Amma swung open vigorously. Amma said, "My son, meditating all day long." A Western man sitting in full lotus with his back to the door remained motionless and absorbed in his contemplation. The next door swung open with Amma's strong push, and she said, "My son, not feeling well, resting now," and she gave a comforting caress to him. Also a Westerner, his face was glowing with peace, but his appearance was pale and thin. He sat up painfully to offer his pranam to Amma; he smiled at us, saying we could meet later in the day.

The last door swung open and inside was a simple cot with a few straw mats on the floor. Amma sat on the cot and asked me to sit next to her. She took my hands and turned them palm up. She studied one, and then the other. She didn't seem satisfied, so she asked, "Which one for ladies?" No one had a particular opinion about it, so Amma took up my left hand. I knew that there was no life line on my hand, or at least not much of one. Maybe that was what Amma had been scrutinizing? The next thing I knew, Amma, with her own thumbnail, was pressing hard on the place where my lifeline fizzled out. She held her thumbnail there for a long moment, and then released my hand from hers. As the coming weeks passed by, I noticed a faint, new line forming where Amma had pressed. A short diagonal joining to another nearby line, extending my lifeline considerably. That diagonal joiner is still visible on my left palm to this day.

Next, the music lesson began. First Amma wanted me to try, "Hamsa Vahana Devi," but the ...*akhila loka kala devi amba saraswati*... line was clearly too much for me. Amma immediately switched to "Devi, Devi, Devi, Jagan Mohini." Those lyrics I could sort of manage. Again, I was encouraged to hold the notes and not let my voice waver so much. It was great fun for everyone! Although feeling a little embarrassed, the overriding emotion was one of a warm welcome and immediate acceptance. These were kind people, comfortable and relaxed.

Now it was lunchtime. Amma led us to her family home adjoining the Kalari. More people had come for lunch, but we all fit in the main room easily. Plates and cups were put out, straw mats were spread, and Amma went around to serve rice and dahl on each one's plate. A small dab of vegetable was carefully given. A warm pink colored herbal tea was poured into the cups, and someone said something like, "*karangali vellum*," thinking that might mean something to me.

Then a beautiful chanting began that went on for some minutes. A concluding touch was the pouring of a small amount of water into the right palm, while chanting a short verse, and then the water was sprinkled in a clockwise direction around the plate of food. It made me feel peaceful. The meal was so simple and delicious, but I had never eaten so much rice with so little sauce. I did not want to ask for more sauce as the pot seemed small and already quite empty.

Amma sat with us, but did not eat. She talked in a most animated way. At one point she came over to pull on my right ear for some reason. Great laughter erupted. I couldn't believe how at ease I felt with this circle of strangers all having a chuckle at my expense. Actually, I was laughing too as the feeling of mirth was contagious. Thankfully someone thought to translate. "Amma says your face is familiar to her. The mark on your ear is where she pulled on it the last time for some mischief you caused." Hmmmm. What could that mean "the last time"? And it is true, there is a particular feature on my right ear that was there from birth.

For no apparent reason a forgotten memory came back to me. Growing up, for breakfast, I would always ask for rice with a pat of butter on it. My brothers and sisters were all eating Lucky Charms and Fruit Loops, but my poor mom had to boil rice for my breakfast. Things were falling into place. The meal finished and Amma took leave.

MY FIRST ARCHANA

I slept for nearly 14 hours before being awakened by the ringing of a bell. My travel clock read 4:00 am. A schedule pasted to the wall of the room listed: 4:30 am — Archana. Whatever that meant, I wanted to be there. After pouring some fresh water from the bucket over myself for a bath I headed out into the cool, dark, pre-dawn morning.

The meditation hall was the room underneath Amma's upstairs apartment. It measures roughly 15 by 20 feet. Through the window I could make out a dozen or so figures sitting silently. It looked like there might be just enough space for me to sit near the door without disturbing anyone. So I tiptoed in and started to settle in that spot when I noticed that everyone was shifting to make space for me. How courteous they all were, the monks. In less than a moment the entire wall to the right of the entrance was completely empty. They had rearranged themselves in a very tight compact size on the far side of the room. Now I had more than one quarter of the whole room all to myself! As I was the only female present it seemed that they must be leaving space for the other two girls who lived in the ashram. Little did I know that I had invaded their space!

Oblivious, I settled in, tucked my leg up in half lotus, and tried to manage in the simple dress I was wearing to sit properly. No one was looking my way, that was for sure, so it was easy to relax and focus.

The chanting began and was in Sanskrit, which was totally new to me, as was formal meditation. But I was eager to learn about it all, so I sat with closed eyes and went with the vibration of the rhythmic intonations. My mind was getting refreshingly soothed when I noticed a distinct increase in the intensity and focus of the archana.

A deep voice, rich in overtones, had just joined and I peeped open my eyes. It was Amma! How lovely that she did the archana too! And look, no book like the others had. She knew this one by heart! No one had told me to expect Amma, so it was thrilling to see her wearing a silky white, floor-length cloth tied at the nape of her neck with her hair wrapped in a bun on top of her head. She was scintillating with energy as she sat on the floor beside the rest of the group on a simple carpet. So much energy flooded the room suddenly. Not to disturb the flow of it all, I closed my eyes and became absorbed in the sound vibration. For no apparent reason, tears welled up in my eyes and my heart filled with a warm, loving sensation. Maybe my soul recognized the "1000 Names of the Divine Mother," as if meeting a friend after a long time away.

NAMES FOR BREAKFAST

After the archana, everyone dispersed out into the coconut grove for an extended period of meditation. I found a quiet spot and tried to go for it too. As I had never been instructed in meditation, I imagined that it might be difficult, but Amma's blessing must have been there because my mind sank like a stone into a deep stillness. Complete silence enveloped my mind and my awareness sharpened. How long I sat, I do not know. But then a bell rang and my senses returned. Standing up, I brushed off the sand and went back to the family house. There was a steaming pot of rice gruel being served on steel plates.

A small bowl to the side had salt in it. It was a breakfast reminiscent of my childhood.

After washing up, a Western female resident approached me. She was so nice and welcoming, asking Flora and me to carry Amma's breakfast tray upstairs. So off we went. The door was open and Amma was sitting on the floor with her hair down looking unbelievably radiant. Amma was just overflowing with shine! She looked up at us and turned to a couple people sitting with her and exclaimed, "Kusuma and Kushula!" Everyone shook their heads with a kind of recognition and one monk translated. "Amma says you are 'Kusuma,'" pointing to me, "and you are 'Kushula,'" pointing to Flora. He then explained that these were two names that appear in sequence in the archana. "Those are your new names!" he said. Everyone looked so happy, and Amma motioned for us to join them. I noticed that Amma's breakfast did not look much different from ours! Just one additional bowl of boiled tapioca root and a small dish of bright red chutney. Amma began distributing the tapioca to everyone, and then continued discussing some topic we had interrupted with our entrance. The mood was relaxed and animated.

Later that morning I was asked to register with the 'Office,' which meant sitting in a small side room of Amma's family house to sign into a large ledger and show my passport and visa. The monk now known as Swami Poornamritananda was the one helping me and he asked, "How long will you be staying?" I blurted out my reply,

"Forever!" He looked at me with a puzzled expression. But then shook his head knowingly. "But for now only until the end of my six-month tourist visa." He made a note of that and returned my passport with a smile.

Another small room next to the Office was set aside for a library filled with an exceptional and rare collection of wonderful books many donated by Nealu, the American monk now known as Swami Paramatmananda – the thin man we had met in his hut the previous day. The monk who was the library attendant helped me by finding an English translation of the "Sri Lalita Sahasranama—The 1000 Names of the Divine Mother." I asked him to point out the names 'Kusuma' and 'Kushula.' He told me they were numbers 435 and 436: champeya kusuma priya and kushula – the 'beloved flower Champaka' and 'the clever one,' respectively.

I borrowed the book and began copying the Divine Mother's thousand names into a booklet I fashioned by folding lined paper and stitching in a center seam. My heart was fluttering with excitement. This was a dream come true! The English translations were also there and the task absorbed me for hours. Soon I had my own handmade booklet in English for the morning prayer which would serve as my archana book throughout the early years.

That same afternoon Amma sent two of the Western residents to accompany me into the village of Kayam-kulam to buy saris and some other basic supplies. When Amma had seen that I had brought only a small bag from America she inquired why. I told her that my wish was to wear a sari and so there was no need to pack a big suitcase of things. My plan had been to get everything here. She shook her head side to side in the Indian way of indicating approval. Besides seeing to the purchase of what was needed, Amma also asked the Western woman to help me tie the sari properly. I felt that each detail was important to Amma.

That evening would be my first bhajan session, which I was looking forward to with great anticipation. In those days there were no published songbooks, much less English ones, and no formal recordings. But I had heard one of Amma's bhajans on a scratchy cassette recording that Greg had played during the slide show a few months before. Amma's voice and the melody of that song were captivating, though the words had been difficult to make out. It had sounded something like, "Amme Bhagavad Gita nitya…" I couldn't wait to hear Amma sing in person. So, in my new checkered sari and with my woven asana in hand I took my place on the open veranda in front of the Kalari where all the ashram residents could fit comfortably.

Fragrant incense wafted on a light sea breeze and an oil lamp glowed with a golden light. The sunset colors were ablaze in the sky, where a few eagles could be spotted coasting in the wind. Amma joined us momentarily. She sat facing east, just to the left of the open temple doors. The harmonium player was facing Amma, and the tablas were set up just to the side, also facing Amma. Surprisingly, I found it more comfortable for my eyes to remain closed. It was effortless to become absorbed in the chanting; Amma's singing was so powerful and natural. Her arms were upraised and moved gracefully through the air like the birds soaring overhead. Her face tilted towards the sky, body swaying in time to the melody. Amma was calling out through her singing so fervently that the thought came to me, "No one in the whole world could be calling down the sky like that! Not even Aretha Franklin!"

When the first song ended, Amma leaned forward and said something quietly to the harmonium player. Much to my surprise and delight he played the opening notes to the song I had heard in New Mexico:

amme bhagavati nitya kanye devi,
enne kataksippan kumbitunnen

O Auspicious Mother, the eternal virgin Devi,
For Your glance of grace I bow down.

maye jagatinte taye chidananda
priye mahesvari kumbitunnen

O Maya, O Mother of the World,
O Pure Awareness! Pure Bliss!
O beloved Great Goddess, to You I bow down.

I was swept away, overcome with emotion hearing Amma sing that song, the very song which had called me halfway around the world to meet the Goddess with the blazing, starry eyes. How could she pick that song? Was it just a coincidence? Out of nowhere, a single thought entered and became fixed in my mind. There was nothing more for me to seek. My determination to find the Ancient Mother in this world had been fruitful beyond my wildest dreams. Tears streamed down my cheeks, and there was no more need to be filled. Every part of my being was satisfied. I felt no doubt.

DAY THREE

Archana was even more wonderful with my new handwritten booklet. However, that morning Amma did not join us, which made me aware how special the morning before had been. But good fortune was with us as, upon exiting the hall after the archana, Amma could be seen a short distance away in meditation under a coconut tree in the front yard. Following the lead of the others, each sitting in different spots, I kept a respectful distance and settled in. For some reason it was so easy to slip into a deep meditation without ever having practiced meditation before. I knew it must be Amma blessing me, as my mind was usually jumping around like a monkey. When we joined Amma, it was still dark and the next thing was the chime of a bell calling us to 9:00 am breakfast.

Where had the time gone?

After breakfast, Amma was roaming around, and she called me to join her, "Kusumam," with such tenderness I felt a pang in my heart.

Through a translator I asked if I could help with some of the ashram chores. Amma's face lit up. She took

my hand in hers and we set off, heading for the kitchen. Amma called out some directions and a pile of vegetables appeared, a few knives and one cutting board. A big, empty cooking vessel was placed next to Amma. I got the cutting board and Amma, with incredible speed and dexterity, began cutting vegetables in her cupped hand. The miniature machete that she deftly wielded could not be easily seen, it moved so fast. How could anyone cut veggies that fast?

I marveled as Amma's pile was 10 times bigger than mine after only five minutes. She was fixed on the task, but also eliciting laughter from the others who had gathered to watch. At one point Amma turned to me and spoke a few words, which were translated by one of the monks. "Amma says a small tree needs a fence around it for protection. So it can grow. Otherwise the cows will eat it." I took that in and knew that Amma was encouraging me to converse with her. I felt touched by what Amma had said and fell silent. It had never been so fun cutting vegetables! And then it was done.

Next we moved onto pot washing. We dragged the big rice pot out and a few other vessels to a water tap behind the kitchen. A bowl of ash and a couple of large wads of coconut fiber were the only necessary tools to get the job done. Unbelievable how clean you could get the pots using only ash mixed with sand. By lunchtime it was decided. I would be the pot washer. For the next six months, after every meal or milk-water preparation, I would come to the back door of the kitchen to collect the dirty vessels and return them clean and shiny. I was thrilled!

DEVI BHAVA DARSHAN

The next day was Sunday, my first Devi Bhava Darshan. A large number of people had arrived in the afternoon, and the atmosphere was very festive. After Amma led the bhajans at sunset, she entered the Kalari and the temple doors were closed. A resident informed me that I could sit inside if I liked and was shown the place to stand so as to be one of the first to enter. Everyone was singing their hearts out when the temple doors were thrown open. Amma was waving a lamp that burned brightly with fragrant camphor. A silver crown and other items I could not recognize decorated a small stool in the center of the temple. The song Amma sang was "Ambike Devi," the same song Amma still sings before sitting for the Devi Bhava:

> *ambike devi jagannayike namaskaram*
> *sharma dayike shive, santatam namaskaram*

> O Mother Ambika, O Leader of the World, salutations!
> O Shive, who gives happiness; forever, salutations!

> *shanti rupini sarva vyapini mahamaye*
> *antadi hine atma rupini namaskaram*

> O Thou whose form is peace, who is omnipresent,
> O Great Deluder!
> Without beginning or end, Your very form is the Self,
> I bow to You!

Before the song was finished, the doors closed again and the intensity of the music increased. Not knowing what to expect, I was chanting my mantra and had my eyes glued to the temple doors. Before long they again opened, but this time Amma was adorned in the most beautiful way imaginable. My heart spontaneously overflowed with love and some ancient memory. Seated on the small stool now, wrapped in a shimmering emerald-green sari, Amma held a sword in her right hand and a trident in the other, both resting on her knees. The jingling of anklets could be heard intermingled with the sound of the mantras being chanted, the conch blowing and the temple bell ringing. Amma's eyes were closed for a moment and then opened. Standing only a few yards away from Amma just at the side of the temple door, a wave of heat and light washed over me that cannot be described. Her eyes were dazzling pools of love and peace. The whole apparent world had disappeared; for me, there was only Devi. Someone nudged me to go inside the temple and I touched the threshold with my right hand as someone had shown me to, and stepped in.

The energy inside the temple was about 1,000 times more powerful. Amma's whole body was subtly vibrating and the air itself felt surcharged with electricity. Placing my asana along the wall just to Amma's left and a bit to the front, I sank to the floor. One of the Western female attendants was seated to Amma's immediate left assisting with various tasks. Amma looked over at me and smiled;

my mind melted. My eyes closed and I sat. At one point someone came to whisper "dinner" in my ear, but it was as if hearing it from a faraway place, not connected to my own sense of hearing. Maybe Amma told them not to disturb me again because more time went by. In fact, the whole night had passed before a hand gently touched my shoulder and somehow I knew to get up. Amma was moving around inside the temple. She stopped and stood in front of each person who still remained inside, perhaps 10 or 12 of us, to give a final embrace.

Amma came to me last. She placed her hand on my shoulder and gazed deeply into my eyes for a long time. Her eyes emitted so much power and light. Whatever you call that transmission, it penetrated to my core and stilled my thoughts completely. My mind fused in that moment, drinking in all the love being poured out. When she embraced me it was all I could do to stay standing.

"YOU HAVE THE SAME POWER"
The Kalari
December 1983

Each Tuesday, Thursday and Sunday night it became my habit to sit in that spot to meditate for the whole Devi Bhava, only getting up at the very end for Amma's last hug. On those nights I would not eat dinner. One such night it was nearing the end when I sensed some stirring at the temple door. Looking up, I was horrified to see a man, more dead than alive, standing there waiting to

enter. His whole body was covered with wounds, some
open with pus oozing out, his eyes were retracted into
the eye sockets filled with mucous, his ears were withered
away with wounds and his head had no hair, swollen like
an overripe melon. I don't need to say that the smell was
very strong. The urge to faint and vomit came to me at
the same time. Certainly someone would prevent him
from entering the temple!

Quickly glancing to see Amma's reaction, my mind
could not reconcile what I saw. Her face was melting with
love, as if her favorite, long-lost relative had appeared on
the scene. She beckoned him into the temple, into her
open arms. He rested his head on Amma's shoulder just
as each devotee had done throughout the night. Amma's
face was beaming with love, even more than I had seen
before. Putting sacred ash into her hands, she soothed his
arms and back over and over again, all the while speaking
to him in a soft, tender voice, consoling him. For his part
he stood mutely with his disfigured head hung down yet
completely relaxed while Amma took care of him. Remember that I was sitting less than three feet from this
scene, and the full visual effect on me was unnerving, to
say the least.

But the most intense part was yet to come. Apparently
not satisfied with her effort, Amma now turned the leper
around so that his back was to her. Some of the worst,
most active wounds were on his upper back. Amma pulled
him towards her and with her mouth began gently sucking

the pus out and spitting it into a small brass bowl which her attendant held close by. The look on Amma's face was one of pure intention. There was not a trace of repulsion or any hurry to finish a distasteful task. The mood was that Amma had all the time in the world for this person. Then with her tongue she licked the worst wounds and ran her forefinger along the fissure as if to seal up a seam. And that went on for some time. Finally Amma gave him *prasad*, holy water and a banana and stood up, ending the Bhava Darshan.

For the next couple of days my mind was in a state of shock. Being trained in environmental science at UC Berkeley, I was absolutely unable to grasp how it was that Amma was doing what she was doing. A few residents tried to answer my questions. The monk who is now Swami Amritaswarupananda explained that the leper had been coming for some time, his name was Dattan. The monk now known as Swami Amritatmananda said Amma was healing him, he was much improved from his former state. Their answers increased the reeling of my thoughts. I decided to approach Amma about it.

It was mid-morning when I found Amma gardening with a large hoe. She was making water wells around the coconut trees in the front yard. The circle she was forming around each tree to act as a shallow bund was perfect in its form. It reminded me of the symbol on the black granite at the entrance of the path leading to Amma's home.

Through a translator I requested Amma's permission to ask about the leper. She put down the hoe and gave me her full attention.

"Amma, what I saw the other night is not possible, I mean scientifically possible. Such diseased tissue cannot be regenerated. How is it possible?"

"Daughter, do you want to know the miracle?"

"Yes, Amma, please tell me."

"The real miracle is that you have the same power inside of you, but you don't know it. Amma has come for (showing you) that."

She smiled a gentle smile, picked up the hoe and resumed working with the trees. Amma was not going to make a big deal about the fact that she was healing a leper! There was not a trace of ego or pride. From Amma's point of view, the extraordinary action I had witnessed was significant only to the extent that it served as a stepping-stone for Self-discovery. In that moment something galvanized inside of me. All former reference points of my life disintegrated. An irrevocable, tectonic shift occurred in my worldview. My heart opened up to this beautiful, humble divine being who wanted only to show me what was inside of my own heart.

There and then I dedicated myself to stay with Amma and learn from her what there is to know. It was one of those moments in life when you know. You just know. Your heart knows with absolute certainty. And we step forward from that point, never to be the same again. To be remade in that moment of hearing, of witnessing. A heretofore unknown resonance was echoing in the deepest chamber of my heart, setting me on the spiritual journey I continue on today.

For 29 years I have meditated on the image of Amma opening her arms to the leper Dattan. Looked at it from almost every angle. Imagined myself to be him, to tune into his experience of emerging from death to life because of the mercy of the Divine Mother. Imagined my own arms taking him in. Impossible. Luxuriated in the memory of the intense, incandescent beauty of pure love that was on Amma's face as she received the leper into her arms. And what is the recurring message? That the love was of far greater importance than the healing from Amma's point of view.

Furthermore, all of us have the power of that Supreme Love inside of us. Call it God's Love, Divine Love, or *Prema* (Supreme Love) in Sanskrit; whatever one chooses to name it, it is all-powerful, ever-victorious, eternally universal Love. According to the saints and sages from all traditions, this love is our own true nature, we are just cut off from it. The goal of spiritual life is to awaken in that Supreme Love which is our innate nature; our inherent and greatest potential as human beings.

Who has the power to give life to the dying? The one in whom is vested that power need not soil their beautiful silks embracing a rotting man. It is enough if they show their palms to him and beam the healing through the power of their mind. They have that power. But for Amma to show Dattan, a man who had been rejected by his own kith and kin and left to die, that he was loved was the more powerful of the two possibilities. Who has a mind which conceives of that? Who is the arbiter of destiny? She walks among us, and her name is Mata Amritanandamayi. The Mother of Pure Grace. 🪔

CHAPTER TWO

Getting My Feet Wet

As it is nowadays around Amma, so it was then. In a single day there can be so many experiences and those early months flew by. The ashram routine was pasted to the wall of my room and served as my daily guide.

4:30 am: Archana
6-9 am: Meditation/Yoga
9 am: Breakfast
10 am: Scriptural Class
11 am-1 pm: Meditation
1 pm: Lunch
2-4 pm: Free time
4-5 pm: Class
5-6:30 pm: Meditation
6:30-8 pm: Bhajans
8:30 pm: Dinner
9-11 pm: Meditation

My first big discovery was that I loved to meditate. Everything else fit into my day around the meditation sessions. Mainly I sat on the verandah of the Kalari. For hours. That way meals, class, and pot-washing were only a couple of steps away. Efficient, not in anyone's way, entranced. Having roused myself to eat meals or wash pots, I would wander back to the Kalari and settle again. Like that the days, then weeks and months passed.

CLASS TIME

Classes were a special highlight of the day; Bhagavad Gita in the morning, and one of the Upanishads in the afternoon. I remember one particular morning when a new class was being inaugurated by Amma herself. She sat in the Vedanta Vidyalayam, a small open shelter with a simple roof and concrete floor just caddy corner to the west side of the Kalari. Seated on a small raised platform with a stack of books beside her, Amma lit the ornate oil lamp used on such occasions as the monk who was taking the class led the chanting. Amma threw flower petals onto the books and onto us and blessed a *kindi* (ceremonial brass pot) of water which she sprinkled all around. Then, one by one, each of us proceeded towards Amma, offering a deep pranam and receiving the new book from her hands. I looked at my book. The title read, *Vedanta-Sara*, by Adi Shankaracharya.

Studying Vedanta was an eye-opener for me. In minute detail, Adi Shankaracharya explained the philosophy of oneness, of a unified field of pure consciousness, of pure existence, of Brahman being the substratum of the universe. To directly experience the oneness, to go beyond our apparent reality, is inherently possible if we set ourselves to the task. It is the goal of human birth. The experience is

not to be attained; we already exist in that state. However due to our lack of understanding, we identify ourselves with our bodies and minds, which are transient, and not their eternal substratum — pure consciousness. We must understand that all sensual pleasure is ephemeral and ultimately a source of future suffering. The more clearly we see this, the easier it is to detach from our selfish likes and dislikes. We gradually awaken more and more to a true vision of the world, of ourselves and of God, directly experiencing all three as one pure consciousness in essence. With our vision corrected through spiritual understanding, all of our fears disappear. All of our selfish desires fade away. Thus we are liberated from our selfishness. This doesn't make us inactive, but like Amma we continue to act—not for our own sake—but for the sake of the world. For a scientifically trained mind like mine, Shankaracharya's *Vedanta-Sara* was a balm of pure relief. My mind absorbed his lucid explanation of the true reality as one would drink water after a long walk in the desert.

The other two female residents were from Australia; we were all roughly the same age, though I was the youngest. One was the personal attendant for Amma and the other was the quiet, contemplative type who served Amma during the Devi Bhava Darshans. Each of us was occupied with our particular duties and not a moment of our day was spent in conversation with one another. I got to know them entirely through our time spent side by side doing service for Amma and the ashram.

I admired them both: they had a special air about them of always seeming to know the right thing to do. One was constantly chanting her mantra, silently of course, while attending to Amma's immediate needs such as cooking, cleaning and washing clothes. She was very efficient in her duties, but also found time to give me special tasks to do that brought me close to Amma.

The other woman was equally gifted with efficiency in the scholarly department. I noticed that after each class while I was parking myself for a meditation session, she returned to her room, diligently copying out her class notes into a large ledger-type book and inserting the Sanskrit and English translation of each verse about which we had just been lectured. What I had accomplished at university in the sciences, she was transacting in the scriptural realm. Her focus and love for Mother during Devi Bhava was amazing. She remained quietly present at Amma's side, never missing a beat until the very end, which was usually 3:00 or 4:00 in the morning.

I wondered if I would I ever have such qualities of self-discipline. I soaked in the spiritual concepts we were learning in class and performed selfless service through pot washing, but the core of my spiritual practice was my time in meditation.

A YOGA SESSION

One morning Amma called me to her room shortly after breakfast. Someone had mentioned that I knew hatha yoga and she wanted to see my *asanas* (yoga poses). A couple of residents were sitting quietly in the corner not paying much attention to me. So I began, starting with the Sun Salutation. Then stood in the Archer Pose on one foot for a long time. Then up on my head for a headstand and some other poses Amma requested. I didn't think much of my yoga practice as I had learned casually from a high school friend's mother who had showed me the basics. But Amma loved it, having me repeat certain poses over and over again.

Finally Amma asked me to sit facing her in full lotus. That was easy enough. Amma also assumed the full lotus position, aligning her knees with mine. That was when the fun began! Amma reached forward and grasped my forearms. I reciprocated. Then, in a clockwise rotation we began making a slow circle, first small, then the arc grew bigger and bigger. Soon Amma was sweeping backwards just above the floor level, as I was leaning forward to counter balance Amma's weight and force of movement. Then my torso circled backwards, just above floor level, barely angled enough to keep from touching the floor, but Amma's weight and swing counterbalanced me.

Amma, through her grip, indicated to go faster. So, round and round in this swirling motion we went in perfect rhythm. I had never done this before; it was beyond exhilarating. The attendant was kneeling nearby and I could hear her saying, "Be careful, you are going to bump heads! Be careful! Stop now!" But I knew that

Amma and I were in perfect synchronicity, since when she was circling backwards, I was circling forwards. Anyway, there was no slowing down, as Amma was driving, not me! Finally, Amma did slow down and we all collapsed in a fit of laughter. My head was not spinning at all, but my soul had definitely been spun!

After catching our breath, Amma instructed me to begin teaching yoga to the other female residents. The class would be held in Amma's room in the morning after she went downstairs. And so the first yoga class for women at the ashram was inaugurated by the universe's greatest yogini, Amma!

LEARNING TO DO LAUNDRY

Behind Amma's family house there were three washing stones and a water tap that sometimes even put out water. That is where I found myself the first week, struggling with my laundry. This big washing stone thingy, how exactly did it work? Armed with my bucket, a bar of Rin soap and lots of spots on my clothes, I went at it. Obvious, right? Fill the bucket, soak the clothes, rub the soap, scrub with the plastic brush the places that really needed it, try not to splash your neighbor, and definitely, don't waste water.

Things seemed alright at first, I mean the cycle was going on, but I was really taking a lot longer than the others. Not wanting to be thought of as the wash-stone hogging newbie, I watched what the others were doing while waiting my turn for the water tap. Aha! They were beating their cloth on the stone, and then rubbing it on the surface of the stone. Much more efficient than my tiny scrub brush. So, after replenishing my wash water, I started doing the same. Or I thought I was.

Finally one of the monks, now known as Swami Amritaswarupananda, turned to me and very politely said, "If you bash your clothes on the stone like that there will be nothing left of them. See, try more like this." I was really touched that he wanted to help me improve my technique and didn't mind saying so. He was right, there was a small flicking of the wrist that twisted the cloth in the air so that it came down on itself, and not so directly onto the hard stone. Clearly the cloth was scrunched up more with that movement, which is how the dirty spots got loosened from the fabric. So much quicker too. Only half as loud, and significantly less soap bubbles flying through the air onto the neighbor, which is really poor etiquette. Before you knew it my whole bucket was finished and the next person very appreciatively took their turn.

NIGHTTIME DUTIES

At night after bhajans it became my task to trail behind Amma carrying a flask, a hand fan and a face towel. If it happened that Amma would ask for a particular item, I would run to get it. If Amma called someone, I would go to find them. Amma would roam around, sometimes alone, but more often in the company of devotees who had arrived or with residents. Sitting under the coconut trees, or on the doorstep of the huts, long discussions would go on into the night. Sometimes Amma would playfully laugh and joke around; at other times serious matters were discussed. For me, it was a time of continuous mantra japa and observing what Amma needed. Her energy level never waned; her attention was on the cares and concerns of others. Her time was entirely given over to whoever had arrived to seek her out. Foregoing her own food and sleep, day-in and day-out, it was hard to keep up with her, even for a 23-year-old!

One night after bhajans someone brought Amma a tamboura, the four-stringed musical instrument that has a resonant drone as its sound. Amma began to play the tamboura while gazing at the stars. As I watched her face she slipped away into *samadhi*. I had never witnessed someone actually going into this state, and a wave of purifying peace arose. I did not want to disturb this moment of pure bliss by staring at Amma. But her face was glowing with a moonlit incandescence that seemed to emanate from within. The splendor of Amma's glow was becoming more and more pronounced. Tears silently streamed down her cheeks for some time. Then a soft, murmuring laugh could be heard that sounded as if it came from another plane of existence. It continued for quite some time and then subsided. That was the night I realized this path of love was much deeper than I had imagined. Amma's consciousness was absorbed for hours. I sat close to Amma until she opened her eyes, just before dawn. The monks sat nearby in meditation as the night passed, basking in the sublime atmosphere.

EVERY NIGHT

Every night Amma would call one or two of the girls to stay over in her room to help out. In my opinion, if you want to know what type of person someone really is, go to their room. Mine is messy; Amma's is simple beyond belief. Measuring 15 feet by 20 feet at most, with plain-white paint on the walls, it consists of a narrow cot with sliding-door cabinets underneath where Amma's clothes were kept. No furniture, not even a chair. Amma would sit on a straw mat on the floor for meals. No phone, no TV, just a ceiling fan. The 'kitchen' consisted of a two-burner stove on a tiny balcony, plus a miniscule fridge. The only adornments were a painted clay Krishna statue in one corner and a picture of the Goddess Saraswati, hanging on the wall at the foot of Amma's bed.

At the risk of jumping ahead in the story, I want to share an anecdote. One recent summer while away on tour, a beautiful new room was built for Amma at the seaside. Big, airy, full of light, overlooking the Arabian Sea, fresh ocean breezes, only the sound of waves breaking, a proper kitchen. When Amma arrived back from the tour, she refused to set foot in the new apartment, saying her original room was just fine. And that was the end of that. Amma's apartment that was then, is the apartment that is now, with the addition of a phone of course!

But I wander. Nighttime in Amma's room was a quiet time; I would serve Amma a simple dinner while she read her stack of mail, then wrote replies. But some nights were also when Amma got work done. A common scene was one of Amma reading a letter in one hand, one person reading out another letter. If someone came into the room, the letter reader might pause. Then Amma asked why they had stopped. "But I have two ears, no need to stop." And it was true. Her mind could be fully present in each of the tasks and complete them with perfection.

This was also a time for sorting out any problems if residents needed counsel or correction. Amma had an "open-door policy," which meant the apartment door was kept open. We could pop in at any time if need be. It always amazed me that, day or night, Amma had no need of privacy; the entirety of her time was given to others. If Amma's feet or calf muscles were aching I would rub them, or help prepare Amma's food. "Sleep" was not a word I would use to describe what Amma did when she laid down. It was more to rest her body for a few hours. Her awareness of all that was going on continued even during this time which was evident because many times she would wake us up to take care of someone who had arrived in the night, or had fallen ill and needed help.

COOKING FOR AMMA

Once I was asked to prepare a side dish for the dinner tray. The other person who usually cooked for Amma recommended which dish to prepare and gave precise instructions. But instead of chanting my mantra without interruption, I remember thinking, "Oh, how lucky I am to be making this dish! Amma will enjoy it so much. Maybe I will be the one she always asks to cook for her!" Pure ego went into the dish instead of pure mantra.

Dinner was served, but I was called away for some other duty. Disappointed not to get the opportunity to watch Amma enjoying my offering, little did I know what was about to happen next. About a half an hour later someone came running to get me. They were calling me to Amma's room as she was feeling extremely sick. When I reached there, I was horrified. Amma began violently throwing up in the bathroom and she wanted me to hold her steady. I felt so bad as I stood by Amma's side to help her and pour fresh water, and offer her a glass of water to rinse her mouth and give a towel when the nausea had subsided, as it eventually did. I knew it must have been from the dish I had prepared with so much ego. What a disaster!

The monks were very concerned to know how I had prepared the food and why had I given that particular dish which was usually not to be eaten at night. So, after Amma had gotten it out of her system, we all sat together. I told everyone what the real problem with the dish was, and waited for Amma's response. She burst out laughing and pulled my ear, my right ear of course, the one she pulled on the day we met. She told everyone, not just me, that we needed full awareness when performing each and every action. The mantra would help us if we chanted continuously. It would purify every action if we chanted with *sraddha*–awareness and faith.

We all listened attentively, me the most of course, since it was really my moment to learn. This was the way Amma taught, with a gentle ease, not to shame one particular person, but to make sure the essence was conveyed; not only for the benefit of the individual, but also for others. Over all these years Amma continues in this vein. Many a scolding has been doled out, sometimes not immediately obvious why the particular situation was eliciting Amma's strong response. I have noticed that Amma's tone was always at the level of the person who the teaching came to. Those with sharp tongues got sharp rebukes, those more gentle in nature received accordingly. If a scolding seemed confusing, I found that with self-reflection, it always became clear what needed correcting. Amma's task was to free us from our sense of "I"-ness, and "my"-ness, from our petty selfishness. Generally, I needed to lose my sense of doership. Why should I react towards Amma, isn't that what I came for? To become truly free?

LIGHTING LAMPS

On another night after the bhajans, several private cars arrived to transport Amma and the ashram residents for a house call in Kollam. One of Amma's earliest devotee's family home was there, and a reception had been arranged. It was already 9:00 pm when we piled into the cars—Amma and the girls in the back and two monks in the front. The other cars were packed with all the rest of the residents and the instruments. When we got into Amma's car, the backseat was quite cramped. I was able to crouch down without too much trouble, leaving more room for Amma, plus a perfect view of the scene that was unfolding. Amma began singing "Siva Siva Hara Hara," and what started out slowly soon became a full speed bhajan that was not ending. Amma was laughing and calling out; we were all singing fully from our hearts. The whole car was imbued with an indescribable bliss. I don't know how the driver managed! When the song ended we were practically in Kollam. Amma's mood had become very exalted and animated. Her eyes were burning embers.

I asked Amma about the intense bliss I felt while singing a bhajan with my whole heart, which only happened sometimes of course. "Is that true bliss?"

Amma told me to keep trying to narrow the gaps between the moments when I experienced that bliss, to make it continuous. Then that would be the true experience, when all the gaps were gone. By the time we reached Kollam, it was clear that we were in for a special night.

The home was decked out for Amma's arrival. Strands of flowers were streaming all around the veranda and an enormous oil lamp burned brightly at the front walkway. Amma was led to the family puja room, where trays of fruits and fragrant jasmine flowers were heaped in profusion. Shining brass puja items were arranged on a tray near where Amma sat. The monks all crowded in. I was sitting just behind Amma with a face towel and fan.

Every single photo on their multi-faceted altar was adorned with fresh flower malas; someone had spent the whole day preparing the prayer room so perfectly. Wherever you looked there was some display of beauty. A large photo of Amma in Devi Bhava occupied the central area. Amma began by lighting the brand new oil lamp from a smaller handheld lamp, which she had lit with a match. Next a few tablets of camphor were lit from the lamp and, with her bare fingers, Amma began floating them on the water in the brass kindi. How could she do that without burning her fingers or extinguishing the flame? As the camphor swirled on the top of the water, Amma took a pinch of sacred ash and sprinkled it into the water. Now the burning camphor drifted and dashed in different directions, Amma watching the movement all the while. The monks were already chanting mantras and Amma joined in after sometime. These were not the mantras I had been hearing at the ashram. They were different. With my lack of knowledge of Sanskrit, they simply became 'the house-call mantras.'

Amma lifted the large vessel of water that she had blessed with the camphor and sacred ash. She held it near her face and breathed onto the surface of the water, and then inhaled the air deeply. At least that is what it looked like from my vantage point. The arati spoon was lit and Amma circled some of the puja photos with the flame, but not her own. She scooped up a handful of jasmine flowers mixed in with some pink and red flowers I did not recognize. She held them for a moment over the burning camphor and then threw them in blessing onto the photos. Sprinkling some of the holy water with her right hand into the room and onto the people in attendance Amma began to sing:

Vedanta venalilute oro nadanta panthannalannal
ni tan tunaykkum avane enne Gitarttham ippozh evite?

Now where is the Truth of the Gita
that proclaims You will guide
a traveler to the ultimate silence
through the dry hot season of Vedanta?

That song was the counterbalance to the bhajan we sang driving in the car. I could feel the bliss of the song beginning to carry me away and tried to do as Amma had suggested. Close the gaps. Still the thoughts and hold the mind on a single point. Dissolve in divine love for at least a moment.

Afterwards the family took Amma to a large room where she could receive the many family members and relatives for her darshan. We were all fed a delicious meal; it was my first full course Indian meal, but it wasn't long before I begged them to stop filling my plate. Everyone laughed as I uttered in Malayalam, "*madi*", which means "enough".

We had spent about an hour at the house, and I thought we would now return to the ashram. But instead of getting

into the car, Amma gestured to me to follow her, and off
we went, down the street at a clip. The monks caught up
just as Amma turned into the next house where there was
a burning oil lamp lit at the front door. The family was
waiting expectantly, and Amma was in their puja room
before they could finish washing her feet. The same scene
repeated itself. But Amma sang a different song:

kotannu koti varshangalayi satyame
tetunnu ninne manusyan

O Eternal Truth, for millions and millions of years
Humanity has been searching for You.

Amma gave darshan to that family and their relatives
as well, then ate a tiny bite of food they offered. Out
the door and into the next home, where the lamp was
lit in the entry way. Like this Amma went on for seven
more houses, with me dashing behind to keep up. She
was very speedy! The monks were in-sync with Amma's
pace, no problem. As we left the last house, I glanced at
my watch. It was nearly 2:00 am. The sky was clear and
the air refreshingly cool. But, wait, Amma was heading
in the opposite direction from where we had started. I
ran to catch up.

Her pace quickened and then a little foot path became
visible. Amma turned onto the path, with me close behind. A moment later a separate street came into view.
More than a dozen houses had lit oil lamps all along the
road stretching out into the night! Amma's exuberance

never waned an iota. She was an overflowing cup of love, bringing joy into each and every home whose lamp had been lit. Her enthusiasm to bring spiritual sustenance to each person who was waiting in anticipation of her arrival was boundless. We arrived back at the ashram just before dawn.

AMMA'S FAMILY

Amma's family was generous in so many ways; I could see that right away. They welcomed me into their home, gave me a room in their house and whatever they had was for the ashram's support, without expecting anything in return. Their family had been through so much as Amma became more and more known for her divinity. Already six spiritual seekers from three continents had arrived on their doorstep to live near Amma! They could have reacted in any number of ways, but they chose to play the role of gracious host above all else. Getting to know Amma's mother and father, her brothers and sisters over all these years; watching them go off to school, earn degrees, marry and raise their own families, start businesses and become successful in their own right has been amazing.

It could not have been easy to adjust to the constant demands of Amma's growing mission right in their own front yard. Again and again they gave up their own homes and land to move a bit further out to accommodate the constant influx of more devotees. Amma's mother and father, brothers and sisters, gave freely for the well-being of the ashram, so that it could grow.

Many nights found them all enjoying the cool evening air and each other's company, chatting and laughing as families do. Everything they had was shared amongst us all, including their entire house, the property, the food and the firewood to cook the food. If someone came in the night, or needed a place to rest, they always made their home available. While some families might have resented the constant intrusions, they were just the opposite. They felt it was their duty to welcome the devotees.

Years later all the pieces of property they had given away were put into trust in the name of the order of sannyasa that Amma has established at Amritapuri. Not a single family member is in possession of any Ashram property, although each of their properties were given freely to the trust without any compensation—not even a single paisa was paid to them for their own land. All the schools, hospitals, and institutions established by Amma are held in trust by the Ashram board of directors. Even Amma's own name is not listed on any deed or title to any Ashram property! Nor does a single family member of Amma's sit on any board; only the sannyasins comprise the board of trustees. How refreshing in this day and age!

When it was time for Amma's niece Durga to be married in May of 1999 there was a lot of excitement as she was the first of Amma's nieces to be married. The family asked Amma's blessing to take out a bank loan in order to make sure that all the arrangements could be made properly. In India the bride's family still undertakes the bulk of the expenses. The marriage was an auspicious occasion for a number of reasons; it was a sign that Amma's family was able to take care of their own needs without relying on the Ashram in anyway whatsoever.

It was a source of family pride for Sugunanand Acchan and Damayanti Amma that all their children and their spouses were college graduates and had been able to marry well and provide for their own families in the midst of the burgeoning ashram community. Before long they would all be running successful businesses, whether it was a dairy or boat building, due to their hard work and natural talents. They invited one and all to the marriage and the large, memorable feast they put on fed large numbers of people, as is the custom in India.

KRISHNA BHAVA DARSHAN

A surprise announcement was made one morning. On Sunday, Amma would give Krishna Bhava Darshan! This was very special for all the devotees, as previously Amma would do both Devi and Krishna Bhava Darshan on the same night, but was not doing that any longer. Word spread quickly, and on Sunday throngs of people arrived to wait for Krishna Bhava to begin. The atmosphere in the Kalari was totally different. Krishna was playful with the devotees, and Devi was serious. Krishna stood on one foot with the other up on a small stool, there was no sitting. Devotees filed into the temple and received their prasad standing up. A bowl of banana pieces was held for

Amma to feed each person who came for darshan. The bhajans were different also, mainly Krishna bhajans, many of which were tuned to lighthearted melodies. Entering the temple to meditate as usual, I did not feel to go for darshan. It sounds terribly strange to say, but my devotion was entirely for the Divine Mother!

Towards the end of the night someone came to call me for darshan as Amma knew I had not yet come, but I told them that my heart only wanted the Divine Mother. As Krishna Bhava drew to a close, Amma came to the temple door to bid farewell to the devotees, many of whom had stayed on. She stepped just outside the temple door and began to dance with her arms raised up and a glorious smile; even Amma's face looked different that night, more boyish and mischievous! The dance went on and on as the bhajan quickened its pace. Now I regretted my decision to not go for darshan, but there was no way to change that now. What a fool I was! As far as I know, that was the last time Amma gave Krishna Bhava Darshan.

SEWING LESSON

One afternoon when I was in Amma's room, she decided to do some stitching. There was a treadle sewing machine in the corner, and we pulled it out a bit to make it more convenient. Then Amma started the alterations she had in mind. Having never seen Amma sew before, I was fascinated with the process. She got a few of her skirts out from the cabinet where her clothes were kept. Amma's nimble fingers began taking out hems with the stitch ripper so quickly it was impossible to follow what was being done. Eyeing the cloth, she set the slippery fabric in place on the sewing machine with no straight pins to mark the adjustments, and began. Amma could sew seams perfectly straight in no time at all, holding the cloth at the right tension, feeding it to the jumping needle, all the while working the foot treadle to power the machine. She was an expert seamstress – that certainly was obvious!

Finished with all three skirts, she put them aside and asked if I liked stitching. I said yes, but I wasn't so good at it. She gave me a needle and spool of thread and picked out a skirt for me to hem. I was trying my best, but it would take an hour at a minimum for me to finish the work. Amma seemed to be in no hurry and watched me attentively. Through a translator she remarked that a needle cost only a few paisa and was an insignificant item, but if we carelessly left it when the sewing was finished someone might step on it. And that could be a big problem. Just because something seemed insignificant, we should always be careful and have awareness. Otherwise a small thing could become a big thing. Amma was teaching me the ABC's of spirituality, but was I able to learn?

PILGRIMAGE TO KANVA ASHRAM

The Ashram librarian at that time was a Westerner who had some connection to the caretaker of the famous Kanva Ashram near Varkkala in central Kerala. Amma suggested that we go on a pilgrimage there with all the ashram residents. So we loaded into a hired bus and set off. My first spiritual pilgrimage with Amma! Upon arrival, our room was allocated; the girls stayed with Amma, all the rest somewhere else. Good fortune to be a girl for once! Then off for veggie chopping and helping with some small tasks.

In the late afternoon we all gathered by the *tirtham* (holy water) pond.

Amma was in her neckcloth, hair in a topknot; Lord Shiva herself was always my impression of Amma when she roamed around like that. Utterly endearing. We sat all together for a beautiful, extended meditation. The atmosphere was so conducive that not even a monkey could resist sinking into the silence. Some snacks and milk water were distributed as we sat in a tranquil, post-meditation state, no need for talk. Amma spoke in a soft, subdued tone for a bit, but there was no translation. And no real need for one, as I was so content just to enjoy the tone of Amma's voice and the soft glow surrounding her in the approaching twilight. I recall singing bhajans there, followed by a simple dinner of kanji, before tucking in for the night. In the predawn hour we were awakened for archana by a bell. Amma was lying down, but not sleeping. It did not seem to disturb her to go out for prayers, though I was quiet as a mouse anyhow.

The day passed as the day before had, lots of chances to meditate, read Vedanta, write in my journal and help

Kanva Ashram, Tirtham Pond

with the veggies and washing up things. But in the afternoon a great thing happened. Amma called the girls to go swimming. That would be all three of us, plus Amma. A very large water tank, not too far away, was the spot for our swim. We had no swim dresses in those days, so we used our underskirts and tied them up over our shoulder on one side. Amma had a full petticoat which was much more convenient. In we went, slowly not to disturb the water at the bottom of the tank. It was deep, so we had to tread water, then swim out a bit, tagging along so as to give Amma lots of space to do what she found relaxing, which was floating in full lotus gazing up at the sky. After a while Amma had us all join hands and swim in a circle, which was really hard. But she wanted us to pull it off. She kept saying, "My three swans, Amma's three white swans!" It was a beautiful moment of sisterhood for me.

Then abruptly Amma changed her mood and asked us to get out of the water. She was really insistent, so we swam back to the edge of the tank and climbed out awkwardly. What we saw when we looked back at the tank made us shudder. What a sight! There were snakes swimming in our direction—a lot. A whole nest of them it looked like, coming to eat Amma's swans. We all shook our heads; once again Amma had saved us!

PILGRIMAGE TO KANYA KUMARI

My visa was expiring in a month, and my money was running low. So, I wrote to my grandfather and asked if he would wire me some money. He was always generous with me, and within a week $300 had arrived. By then my thinking on the money had changed. I didn't really need it, better to give it to Amma for the ashram to buy bricks for a small underground meditation cave they were building directly behind the Kalari. However, when Amma heard of my idea, she suggested that we all go on another pilgrimage, this time with all the residents and devotees who could fit onto a full-size touring bus. Destination: Kanya Kumari!

Word spread of Amma's invitation, and a few days later we were getting on the bus to drive south. Some food was purchased to distribute for snacks along the way, food packets with curd rice and mango pickle were packed from the devotees' kitchens, and big pots were brought so we could cook some simple food on the trip. Amma was so practical; she made even the simplest, mundane undertakings fun!

En route down the coast, we stopped to hike a famous hillside trail called Maruthamalai that wound its way up to a high cliff with a view that took in the Western coastline of the blue jewel Arabian Sea. We climbed for several hours scrambling over huge boulders at times, a steep rocky path through dry-scrub terrain before reaching the summit. Amma climbed barefoot the whole way! Several of the men carried bulky tins of biscuits and snack items on their heads to be served at the top. I couldn't believe they were able to navigate the trail with their loads, but they looked so utterly happy to have such a special task.

When we reached the top of the cliffs, the view was well worth the climb. It was spectacular to see so much of the coast, the quaint valley below, and several prominent temples clearly visible. One of the features of this cliff was its caves. One was right nearby where we had come up the path with a small wooden door locked with a large padlock. I was just next to Amma holding the fan and face towel as usual.

Then Amma pulled an amazing stunt. I don't know if anyone could see or was even watching as Amma's hand darted out and brushed the lock for a micro-instant. Then she turned around and said to a devotee, "Son, can you try to open the lock?" And when he grasped the lock to try, it just opened as if the inhabitant had forgotten to properly close the lock to secure it. I was left rubbing my eyes at that move. Had I imagined it? But not for long, as Amma had already entered the cave and was settling in for a bhajan and a quick meditation. Someone was living in the cave, which was evident by the bedroll, scriptural books and a small writing desk kept neatly near a simple altar for meditation and puja by the looks of it. Somehow it seemed that everyone could fit inside, even though there were in fact far too many people for such a small space. Amma sang "Mano Buddhyahamkara" and then sat quietly, as we all did, for some time. Someone brought a few flowers and water to Amma, from where I don't know, maybe that was in the cave already? The monks chanted mantras and Amma blessed the altar by throwing flower petals and splashing holy water around the interior.

Out we poured from the mouth of the cave. Amma asked one of the devotees to make sure the door was closed securely behind us. I would have loved to have seen the face of the occupant when he returned later in the day to discover someone had paid him a 'house call.'

Reaching Kanya Kumari, Amma sent some of us on the tippy, tossing ferryboat out to the rock where Swami Vivekananda had swum to nearly 100 years before. It was here he had received his vision of the Divine Mother, whose footprint raised up from the rock is still visible today. It is here, at the foot of Mother India that Mahatma Gandhi, among many others, had his ashes dispersed in the confluence of the 'three seas.' There is a strongly held belief that at the tip of India the Divine Mother will always be present, in some form, though sometimes hard to identify. A living legend at the time, Mayi Amma, was staying there and was believed to be that very soul.

Mayi Amma was very, very old. No one could say her age exactly, as she was discovered in the fishing nets of the local fishermen one afternoon some years ago. They took her for dead, but when they brought her body to the shore she sprang to life and walked away. Her attendants were a pack of dogs, who were always vigilant while she kept a fire burning at the tip of India for hours and hours, day after day. She rarely spoke and inhabited a one-room cottage on the beach with no apparent means of sustenance. Many times she could be seen swimming in the turbulent sea out to a remote rock and lying in the full sun for hours.

Amma wanted to pay a visit, and so we all walked the short distance to her hut. Just before we went in, a camera was thrust in my hands and someone said, "Take a picture." I had no particular skill in photography, nor desire to snap a shot, but the directive was so insistent that I stepped in and looked for the best spot to snap from. The room was simple and clean. Mayi Amma was not old, she was ancient. Her skin was a dark shade of wrinkled leather. She was reposing in a chair with her legs extended on the planks that were attached to the side of this style of chair for that very purpose. She was wearing the dress of a fisherwoman; a plain cloth tied as a skirt and only a shawl covered her upper body. Her white hair was neatly combed; on the crown of her head rested a single white jasmine flower. How did it stay perched there? I thought to myself.

Amma sat on a cot just next to Mayi Amma's chair; the mood was extraordinary, sublime. Silently we all stood scattered around the room, six or eight of us, taking in the scene. I was frozen to a spot on Mayi Amma's right, facing Amma with the camera awkward in my hand and a very dry mouth. How on earth could I possibly have the nerve to "take a picture" and disturb the perfection of the moment? So, I simply stood there like a pillar. Some time passed, and Amma was glowing with a faint blue light and a certain smile I had never seen before. A random thought passed through my mind, "Who on earth is this old woman?" And the exact moment when the thought was complete, Mayi Amma turned and looked directly into my eyes. Clearly she had heard my thought! My breath caught in my throat, and I took in her gaze. What incredibly clear and beautiful eyes! And in her eyes, which were an incongruent deep blue, I saw the ocean. The vast ocean, roiling and moving and alive in her eyes. Time was suspended for that moment, and I felt the blessing of her darshan wash over me like a wave. She broke the gaze after what seemed like eternity, though it was probably only for a moment that she had turned to me. Then I did it. I snapped the picture without even thinking. She didn't seem to mind or notice. Then I took one more of her with Amma in the frame, both looking into each other.

THE HEALING OF A CHILD

To tell the story of a powerful healing I received from Amma just before my departure, I must first tell the story of my difficult early childhood. Born in Chicago to young parents, my mom had left Northwestern University to marry my dad, her college sweetheart, who was a popular upperclassman and football player. We moved to Washington DC shortly after I was born so my dad could work as a journalist at the Washington Post. He abandoned my mom and me before I had turned four. One night, he just didn't come home. My mom had to regroup quickly as there was no family or financial support for her in the DC area. We moved back to Pittsburgh to live with my grandparents.

It was 1963 and divorce was still viewed with disdain. Where we lived was a quiet and peaceful suburb, with about six families in the immediate neighborhood. Traditional families. It must have been difficult for my mom to fit in or make friends given our circumstances. I remember one Fourth of July. All of the kids in the neighborhood had decorated their bicycles so that we could have an Independence Day parade on our street and attend a neighborhood picnic afterwards. The whole morning was spent getting my bike ready, but when the time came to pedal off, I couldn't find my mom in the gathering. So I ran back to my grandparents' house to get her. Telling me that she could not go to the parade for some reason that didn't make sense, I ran back and straggled along to catch up with the others. Only years later did it dawn on me that my mom wasn't comfortable or welcome with that group of families. Ours was the 'different' family without a dad. And that made me vulnerable.

Which brings me back to the point. The kids always played in the wooded area behind my grandparents' house or in the backyard of one of the families. It was a safe neighborhood, everyone knew everyone. Behind one of the family's houses there was a little playhouse where many days and evenings passed in pursuit of fun. Though only five years old, I was allowed to go out and play, as long as I was home for dinner.

One afternoon when I went out to play, no kids had come out yet; maybe they were still napping or in town with their families. Heading to the playhouse I noticed a couple of older boys I didn't know. Playing in the sand I was content to wait for the other kids to show up. Chuckie K. was a little younger than me, his brother C. was older. He must have been a teenager as he never played with the kids. They both came into the backyard area, and C. began talking to the older boys who were pointing to me. They approached me and said they were going to play in the playhouse, why didn't I come in. So I did, of course — we played there all the time.

But this was not a game. As soon as we went in, the door was closed shut. The two boys I didn't know were in there too. They were laughing and being very rough, pushing each other around. One of them started to order me around. I started to cry but they pushed me down. Then they did what should never be done to anyone; I was terrified. Screaming and crying. Then they ran out and left me there sobbing. I made it home, but I was a mess.

My grandmother's housekeeper, Mary Abloff, was ironing when I came in the house. She looked up and knew right away something had happened to me. She cleaned me up, but didn't say anything. When my grandma came home from town she got angry that I had lost my hat. "Where is it?"

"I don't know. Maybe at the play house," I stammered.

"Go find it, it's brand new!" she said.

I started crying again. The housekeeper said that she would go with me to look for the hat. She took my hand

and silently led me back. My hat was inside the playhouse, but there was no one there. I didn't say a word, I was so traumatized. It took many years to fully recollect the incident and try to come to terms with it as a young woman.

I credit Amma with the ultimate healing of my heart from that attack. One of the most profound moments I have had with Amma was when she recounted that story back to me. The thing was, I had never told anyone about that incident. Not even my own mom.

Amma had called me to sit with her inside the Kalari the afternoon before I had to go back to the USA because my visa was finished. Amma began by saying that I had an innocent heart. Also that I was a daydreamer when I arrived who had become serious about spirituality over the past six months. That she was happy I wanted to come back to live in the ashram; a sponsorship letter would be given to me so I could return permanently. My heart was so open to Amma, she was giving me everything I wanted.

Then out of nowhere, Amma changed the subject. Referring to the boys who had hurt me when I was a little girl, Amma said they had done something very wrong, and they had suffered for it. But she said that somehow they must be forgiven. That the past is a cancelled check, otherwise what has happened in the past will ruin our mind, it will just pull us down and destroy us.

Listening to the translation, I was stunned. I nodded my head in agreement because I knew what Amma said was completely true. In that moment I also fully got that

Amma knows everything about us, but only reveals it if absolutely necessary. Like the healing of the leper, Amma has no interest in taking credit for anything she does, or for any powers that she has. There is no trace of ego or self-interest at all when it comes to Amma, not even a nano-trace. If she does something, it is for a good reason, a cosmic reason. She is pure grace itself.

She held me in her arms for a long time and soothed my back with her hand. The vivid memory that had been with me since I was five replayed strongly in my mind, as it had countless times before, but for the first time it didn't make me panic. The images, the screams, the shame, arose and faded. I knew that it was Amma's *sankalpa* (divine intention) for me to finally be free. I relaxed and surrendered into her embrace and let myself be healed. The nightmare was over.

Again, who can do such a thing? Who can grant redemption? Who can definitively 'sort out' events in our lives and release us? As in the case of the leper, the manifestation of pure love trumped any biological obstacle to tissue regeneration. We, the curious onlookers, are the ones who are wonderstruck. Amma wants no claim to fame or glory. In the case of my molestation, the pure healing grace was instantaneously transmitted, but the divine love came first. Any impossibility is rendered possible when it follows in Divine Love's footsteps. Who can transact that? Only God, I say without hesitation. In Amma's life story, I have seen too much of it.

One of the most inspiring parts of the Indian spiritual tradition allows for God to manifest in human form to give solace and direction to those who are suffering and crying out. There is a Sanskrit word, *avatar*, just for that exact phenomenon. Why should God be relegated to heaven to rule over human existence from a remote throne? I love the idea of God coming down to earth and moving among us in a human body. It makes sense to my heart.

CHAPTER THREE

Waiting, Impatiently

Touching down in San Francisco was really tough. Deep culture shock even though only six months had passed. But in those extraordinary months, everything had changed. Now America felt like the foreign country.

The Indian Consulate in San Francisco accepted my application for an entry visa, but made only perfunctory statements about the time it would take. The papers would be sent off to Delhi, then they would make their way to Kerala to be verified. No, they could not say when I might hear back. And no, they did not want to keep my passport, it should be sent back to them once the visa was approved. No, definitely don't buy a plane ticket yet. Please don't call us, we'll call you.

I headed back to New Mexico. Within a week I had found a cheap apartment and a job cooking in a restaurant. As I built a beautiful altar for my meditations and pulled the mattress down to the floor for sleeping, a wave of Amma reached me. It will be okay, was the feeling. So, I determined to make the best of my time here. Amma had stressed that she would be with me always, the least I could do was keep up my practice as best I could.

Recalling an incident that had happened a week or so after meeting Amma helped me. I had learned from one of the ashram residents that initiation into the practice of mantra is called *mantra diksha* and is officiated by the Guru. I was uncertain about my mantra now, having received mine on the Colorado River! So, I asked Amma one morning if she could give me a mantra, not mentioning about having gotten one secondhand. Amma chuckled for a moment when they translated my request and said, "But you have already received a mantra from Amma, haven't you?" Amma was all awareness, all the time! Situations like that were constantly happening around Amma, and at a certain point it felt ridiculous to keep saying, "What a coincidence!" Better to accept Amma's omniscience.

The memory of this incident and others like it kept my faith going while waiting for my visa to come through.

As it was, I needed to earn money for my return. Every extra shift I could get at the restaurant; every training that was offered I signed up for to improve my skills and earn a raise. We all know that cooking in a restaurant involves long hours and hard work for low pay, but at least a decent amount could be earned working 40 or more hours a week. I could have moved back to a city and gotten a position working in line with my college degree. But I wanted to be like a bird on the twig, ready to fly the moment my visa was ready. I didn't want to get entangled in city life and the demands of a career. My priority was to earn enough money to return to Amma, and in the meantime, bide my time in the nature that abounded in New Mexico.

I told all my friends, of course, that I had met the Divine Mother and about all the wonderful things that had happened that past year. What exactly they thought of my experience did not matter to me. My faith was in Amma now and didn't hinge on what others thought. There is a beautiful Hanuman Temple in Taos, New Mexico, established by Ram Dass and the devotees of Neem Karoli Baba. I could go there to keep company with others following the path of love. They sang *kirtans* (devotional songs) and the Hanuman Chalisa beautifully, and the temple became a place where I could relax and be at peace. How lovely it would be if Amma could have a place like that here in the US, I thought.

My first paycheck arrived, and I had already decided what to do with it. I immediately had the bank clerk draft a bank check for $1,008 to the M.A. Mission. Off to the post office, writing Amma's address on the envelope with a slightly trembling hand. Would it reach the ashram without being pilfered en route? It was almost everything I had in the account. It was a plane ticket back. But my rent was paid, some food stocked in the pantry, and I was determined to offer my first paycheck. To be able to help the ashram for whatever was most needed would be such a consolation to me while waiting. I paid a little extra to certify the letter and posted it. What a feeling of buoyancy filled my heart when leaving the post office!

One week later the strangest thing happened. I myself got a certified letter! From my grandfather. He wrote that since my return from India I had been on his mind and that he thought maybe I could use a little money to get started again. Enclosed was a check for $1,000.

And so the time crawled past, every month I would contact the Indian Consulate. Each time there was no change in my 'pending' status. I had set aside my plane-ticket money, and had more than enough to live on. The ashram secretary had written back to me, acknowledging receipt of my gift. But added that Amma did not want me to do that again. She wanted me to save my money in a savings account. I might need it, she said, and soon I would be returning and that way I could meet any unforeseen expenses. Considering the meager resources the Ashram had, it was touching that Amma was concerned about my welfare, alone in the US, away from my own family. She certainly was not interested in money, that was clear. So, I set up a saving account for the excess from my pay.

Six months had passed, and my impatience was mounting. My sadhana was nothing compared to being in Amma's presence, and I could feel the world wearing me down. I had many special dreams of Amma: rubbing her feet in one, getting a long darshan hug in another, swimming together in a river… But it was not enough. My heart was filled with sorrowful longing.

Then Amma wrote to me. She was encouraging me to come back, even if it was on a tourist visa. Enclosed in the packet she had sent was one of her linen face towels. It was a jolt of memory, holding her face towel. My mind began weighing the possibility of what it would mean to withdraw my long-term visa application, which I had been waiting months for. The Indian Consulate did not permit you to do both; if a tourist visa was requested, that was the end of the other paperwork. I wavered. Amma was so clear about it, but the idea of having to return to the USA after another six-month 'visit' seemed too unbearable. As I was mulling over my decision something happened that made everything perfectly clear.

PURPLE PLUM SAUCE

One afternoon at the restaurant, I was preparing a plum sauce for the evening meal. The sauce was made from fresh fruit and had to be boiled for more than an hour until it thickened. Then the bright purple sauce was whizzed in a Cuisinart, rendering it perfectly smooth. As I was doing that step, the top flew off the Cuisinart, and the boiling-hot sauce flew onto my face. I collapsed on the floor from the impact of the burning sauce, and my co-workers moved quickly to assist me. One look at me and they knew it was bad. They made a big ice pack and applied it on my face. An ambulance was called and they transported me immediately. By the time we arrived at the emergency room, I had gone into shock. A co-worker had come as my bystander, and a good thing because I could not even speak properly. The pain was agonizing. He explained to the emergency-room doctor what had happened, as they carefully removed the ice pack. I could see by the

look on my friend's face, and the serious expression on
the doctor's face that it was bad. Morphine was ordered,
and I was wheeled into an examination room. A specialist
was summoned. After examining me, the doctor told me
that I had third-degree burns to a significant portion of
my face, but the burning sauce had miraculously stopped
just short of my eyes so my vision was not threatened. He
said that I would be alright, but that I would very likely
need plastic surgery and infection was a real danger. So,
for the next week, the burn would have to be treated with
meticulous care to avoid any complications. He would
see me in one week and sent me home.

This reversal of circumstance stunned me. How precious each moment of life, each moment of health! How
much I had taken for granted. Having been on the cusp
of deciding whether or not to take a tourist visa seemed
like such a luxury now; my hopes were dashed to bits. I
gritted my teeth not to cry. The tears would not help my
burn, and my spirit had to be strong no matter what. It
could have been worse, I reminded myself; my all-knowing
Amma might not have sent me the face towel in advance
of the accident!

When I got home I gingerly removed the dressing.
Refusing to look in the mirror, I placed Amma's beautiful, perfect face towel onto my burned face. Propped up
on pillows, I fell asleep with Amma's mantra on my lips
and an intense prayer for rescue in my heart. That week
went by in a blur. The doctor had given me some special

burn cream but it felt horrible to rub it on the wounds. Actually, it was difficult to use it because it was too thick and when rubbing it on the burn felt terribly painful. So I stuck to the soothing face towel. And waited for the follow-up appointment. I was resolved to stay steady through the process. To achieve that, I thought as little as possible, constantly chanting my mantra, and did not look in the mirror.

LIFE AT A GALLOP

At that juncture, life took off like a horse galloping back to the barn at sunset. The doctor's appointment kicked off with him questioning whether or not I was the same person he had seen in the emergency room one week earlier. Not understanding the point of his question, and shaking my head in the affirmative, he sat down and rolled his chair close to me, examining my face. "How is it possible? I have never seen such a recovery! What did you do?" I couldn't very well explain the exact situation, but said that the cream was really hard to use so I had kept the wound clean as per his instructions. Leaving the burn open to the air with a linen cloth gently laid over to protect it was all I had done. He looked at me in complete disbelief, but what could he say? He wrapped up the exam and explained that in the future the skin in that area would always be sensitive to the sun. Also, over time it may develop a 'blush' to it because all the capillary blood vessels would be regenerating at an adult age, not from birth hence they would be more pronounced. He told me I was a very lucky young lady; he had no inkling how blessed I truly was!

Then, for me, it was decided. Returning to my apartment I called the Indian Consulate. A tourist visa would suffice. I could wait no longer. After an interminable time on hold, the clerk got back on the phone and he sounded a bit befuddled. Why was I asking for a tourist visa when my long-term visa had been approved a few days before? Didn't I want to send my passport in? I found my chair to sit down, as I was feeling a bit dizzy. And so it was that I returned to Amma!

CHAPTER FOUR

Diving In!

J oyousness. One word says it all. Upon my return to the
ashram everything just seemed to fall into place. Part
of the reason for this was that my accident had increased
my inner resolve. It helped me to see how fleeting life
was, how ephemeral. I clearly saw that this moment with
Amma was all I had. My 'long-term' entry visa was only
for one year, and although it could be extended, this time
felt precious and I intended to make the most of it.

All the money I had saved from my job, which came to
a tidy sum, I offered to Amma. She refused every penny,
insisting that I open a savings account in Vallikkavu, the
little village across the backwaters. After some resistance
on my part, I agreed, with the caveat that if the Ashram
really needed something I wanted to help. My room
would be in the row of coconut huts to the northwest
corner of the Kalari. The local variety of coconut huts is
a rectangular structure made of mats of woven coconut
fronds, set one layer onto the next by lashing it in place
with thick twine. The hut's framework for the woven
mats to be lashed onto is bamboo. To live in one of those
huts had been a cherished dream of mine, never expressed
outwardly. Up to this point I had stayed in a room in
Amma's family house. Another change Amma made was

to adjust my daily routine for more balance. Instead of eight hours of meditation, and three hours of seva, those two proportions were reversed.

SPIDERS AND SNAKES

The coconut hut had no fan and was just big enough to spread out two straw mats. It was heaven! In those days, the ashram was surrounded on three sides by backwaters, and this row of huts was at the edge of the western lagoon. Looking out the window, I could see families of ducks paddling by, people in canoes, water snakes, turtles and frogs. I would often see snakes slithering through the rafters of the hut. However I felt it was just as much their home as mine; that's how close to nature I felt living there in that hut. They weren't bothering me, so why should I hinder where they were going?

One night I returned to my hut very late. There were only a few hours left before archana began, and I wanted to get at least some sleep. Glancing at the back wall, which was also made of woven coconut mats, I noticed a big, poisonous jumping spider. It was hard to see because it blended in so perfectly with the coconut mats. Then I saw there were two of them. No... it was actually three. Make that four... five... I stopped counting. I decided to go to sleep. I was afraid that if I tried to hit them with something, they would all jump on me. And there were a lot more of them than there were of me. Thinking about it further would only produce anxiety. Chances are that

I had been sleeping there with them peacefully all these weeks and just had never noticed them before. If it was my fate to be bitten and killed by poisonous jumping spiders, then swatting at them would only hasten my demise. Either it was going to happen or it wasn't. So, I might as well get a few hours of sleep.

I slept without a care, knowing that Amma was watching over me. Looking back, I wonder at the surrender I expressed in those early days. Of course, Amma wouldn't suggest that we leave ourselves in harm's way if we could clearly see we were in danger. After all, it is God who gives us the power to see the danger and the discrimination to avoid it. But in my innocent faith, I felt that Amma would take care of everything. And she did. I woke up the next morning just in time for archana. Later that day, when I told my spiritual sisters about the spiders in the hut, they helped me to clear them out. I could tell they weren't sure whether to laugh at my folly or be impressed by my faith. Finally, they settled on both.

THE ASHRAM COOK

Within a few days of my arrival, Amma asked me to be the Ashram cook. What an incredible honor, I thought. It must have taken 10,000 births to earn that seva! A young Indian girl who had joined the ashram would also help. The kitchen was inside the family house, and food was prepared over open fires kindled on deep, wide counters with built-in chimneys. The cooking vessels were set up

Taking a break from cooking

on stone blocks which could be cautiously adjusted according to the size of the pot. On my first day, Damayanti Amma, Amma's mother, came herself to teach me how to properly light the fire. She started by showing me a simple puja, offering the first trimmed piece of fresh, white coconut into the flames, a prayer, and the ritual sprinkling of water. She was really strict. She showed me how to do the first-thing-in-the-morning-before-sunrise sweeping. How to hand mop the kitchen floor. The vessels were to be kept a certain way. The water kept pure. The stirring sticks attended with care. As she spoke no English, I am sure my training session must have made for an entertaining scene, had anyone been watching.

And so my day began with 4:30 archana, then into the kitchen no later than 6:00. On Bhava Darshan days, standard lights-out time was 2:00 am or later, occasionally midnight. There was strictly no tea or coffee; boiled milk, diluted one-to-one with water and a generous portion of sugar was served twice daily. If I was called to stay in Amma's apartment in order to help, it meant I would only get a few hours of sleep. And Amma never 'slept' really, more like rested her body. She was always present and alert, even when resting. One night Amma had roused us to say that a family had crossed the backwaters and could not find their way in the dark. So we should assist them in getting a room to stay. Sure enough, there they were, meandering on the path, looking this way and that without any idea how to locate Amma's 'ashram,' which was really not much more than her family's house and surrounding compound.

But I digress. Arriving at the kitchen in the predawn hour, the workday began with a quick cleaning, short puja, centering myself, kindling the fire. Portioning out the rice. Separating the grain from the husk on a large winnowing basket. Washing it carefully, so as not to lose a single grain. Not a single grain should be overlooked, that was a sin that brought misfortune. As the rice came to a boil, warm water from the neighboring vessel should be added, not cold, that would cause rheumatism.

The coconuts, if we had any, had to be scraped out on the shredding stool–a narrow stool with a sharp shredding prong protruding from the raised end. A bit reminiscent of my milkmaid days, the fortitude of the forearms being the critical factor in getting 10 coconuts finished quickly.

Breakfast was prepared for the 25 or so residents. The day's meal count would be given sometime mid-morning, but generally lunch was for 50. Dinner on Bhava Darshan nights would be for hundreds, prepared in cooking vessels big enough to lie down in. After lunch was finished being served, there was a break until dinner preparation began. Often, Bhava Darshan dinner would wipe out the entire pantry, and then we residents would be left to eat plain kanji, with no curry, for breakfast and dinner until we could purchase more supplies. Sometimes that would be days later.

Lunch was always rice, a vegetable curry and then a ladle of sambar, rasam, poullishetti or paddapu dahl. None of these required coconut. Although it grew all around us, it was too expensive. The vegetable curry would be carefully portioned out. Many mornings found me harvesting cheera – wild spinach from patches around Amma's family house. It took a long time to cut enough to serve as a lunch dish. Chembu, or elephant-foot root, was another staple; a dirt-cheap vegetable that required slathering the hands with oil before cutting, as it was a skin irritant when raw. Very nutritious of course, but not praised for its taste. Ladyfinger, drumsticks, bitter melon – those we could never afford. Even potatoes were a luxury. My experience cooking in the ashram was the polar opposite to my experience cooking at the restaurant back in New Mexico. To serve others without expecting any reward was energizing! We worked quietly, silently chanting our mantras, striving to follow Amma's instructions to the T.

Sometimes devotees would bring sacks of freshly harvested cheeni, the delicious local variety of tapioca root. That was a special meal to prepare. Often Amma would come to help cut it, as she still sometimes does during the Tuesday program in the Kali Temple. Green cooking bananas, enormous cucumber melons, other types of local roots, cabbages and carrots were our mainstays. One onion was one onion too much. Garlic – out of the question. Salt, of course. Black pepper, cumin seed, dried red chilies in moderation, a pinch of asafetida, fresh tamarind paste, fresh ginger, fresh curry leaves, coriander seed, mustard seed, and one or two green chilies was all we used for spices and seasoning. Every other morning Amma's adorable little brother Kocchupapa, now known as Sudhir Kumar, would poke his head in the back door of the kitchen to see if there was any need for provisions. Then off he would go to the vegetable market some distance away to get what was required.

It was an amazing time, learning how to properly prepare dozens of different dishes, how to stretch a meal for 50 into one for 100, getting all the instructions in a language I didn't really understand.

The grinding stone was the only electric appliance we had. On days when we could have a coconut curry dish, the freshly scraped coconut would be placed in the well of the circular grinding stone. The pestle was placed at an angle to the mortar and chained in place. Then the motor was switched on, spinning the coconut around and around with fresh ginger and other spices, depending on the dish. It could grind everything to a coarse paste in a half an hour or a fine paste after 45 minutes.

Often quality control showed up, that would be Amma! She would arrive unannounced and dip her finger into the paste while the mortar was spinning, and check for taste. If I had put in even one miniscule shallot, a miniature purple onion, Amma would taste it. A clove or two of garlic, forget it. Amma could determine what had been put in the grinder in a nanosecond. At least I had learned to continuously chant my mantra while cooking, and for Amma that was the most important ingredient!

The cook fires were a challenge for a couple of reasons, the main one being finding enough dry fuel to burn. The rib of the coconut palm frond became one of my best friends, although it had to be completely dried in order to burn. I would stockpile whatever I could find and allow it to dry out over time. Monsoon season was especially challenging. We never bought any outside wood – too expensive. One time an old hardwood tree fell, and a man came and chopped it into firewood. I felt a boon from heaven had been given. Any spare time I spent foraging for pieces of dried up coconut husk, twigs, palm fronds… Any wood, dry or wet, was collected and added to the wood pile.

Damayanti Amma was a tremendous help when it came to making sure that I always had firewood. She would always inform me if she had seen any laying around. Her whole soul was dedicated to ensuring that all the residents were fed on time, and that meant making sure that the cook had a supply of dry fuel. Damayanti Amma never showed anything but kindness to me – although I imagine it took a good deal of adjusting on her part to have me in the kitchen. Now that Amma's family understood Amma's mission in the world, the lengths they would go to nurture the fledgling ashram were unbelievable. The family was ready to do whatever was necessary to provide for Amma's devotees, even if it meant working shoulder to shoulder with someone from half-way around the world who didn't know anything.

The second challenge about the fires was the heat. My whole body seemed to react to the strong heat of the fires in the close quarters of the tiny kitchen. I developed heat blisters everywhere, especially my face. On top of that, once the rice was cooked, the kanji vellum (rice water) had to be poured into a smaller vessel. That meant tipping the rice pot at just the right angle where it was perched on blocks above the cook fire. Imagine pouring 10 gallons of just boiled rice water into a vessel on the floor. You couldn't miss, it would be a disaster! The steam and the heat from pouring the water were causing my body to blister. Watching Amma suffer in her body for the comfort of the devotees made me not want to mention my blisters and heat boils. But one day there was an incident that forced me to show Amma my condition.

BUG BITES

I was always careful not to kill any living thing in the ashram, even if it was a bug or spider. But Damayanti Amma had shown me one thing that I had to eliminate from the kitchen if I saw it, the poisonous centipede. It was the flat, shiny brown variety, and about three to five inches long. She said they were really bad, and that I had to watch out for them in the sinks and woodpile. She said they were aggressive and fast; they would run up your leg and bite you in an instant. Very poisonous and painful. So, I relaxed my standard of non-violence; if I found one, that meant its end. I probably killed two or three of them over the course of six months. I always felt bad about it, but I justified my actions, understanding that they were for the safety of myself and others, which was also important. One night when I was asleep in my hut, I awoke with a start, as there was a pinching sensation on my arm near my armpit. The pinching stopped, and I was just dozing off again when an even harder pinch woke me up completely. I was wearing a choli, the blouse worn under a sari, and my right hand went to the spot where the pain was starting to spread. And then I knew exactly what was happening: under the sleeve of my blouse, pinched between my fingers, I could feel something wriggling – a centipede. Yikes! In an instant I had my blouse off, and, sure enough, there the wretched thing was. It dropped to the floor and began dashing towards the edge of the hut. A nearby hand fan delivered a blow, severing it in two. And I swear it ran off in two different directions! The angry welt on my arm was already spreading, causing pain to radiate down my arm and into my neck. I threw on my blouse and a half sari to go for help. There were residents resting at the side of the Kalari, as they had given up their own rooms for the devotees after the conclusion of the Bhava Darshan a few hours ago. I woke them up because I didn't know what to do and didn't want to disturb Amma unnecessarily. Describing what had happened I looked to them for guidance, but they all felt that centipedes were not too poisonous – I would be ok. They said that in the morning we could see how bad the bite was. They gave me some bhasmam, blessed by Amma, to rub on the bite, which soothed it considerably. They were kind and patient with me, even though their sleep had been disturbed.

They were right, in the morning the bite seemed alright. A painful hardened welt where the poison was delivered, but other than that, nothing much. As I am allergic to bumblebee stings, I am aware of bad reactions to insect bites; this was not one. So, off to the kitchen to light the fires. About an hour into the cooking, I had all but forgotten about the bite when a rush of adrenaline went through me. It felt like someone had lit a fire in my bloodstream. Stunned, I sat down on the floor. The young Indian girl who helped in the kitchen could tell that something was seriously wrong with me. She put down the cooking ladle and grabbed my hand to take me to Amma. Amma inspected me and saw two things: welts popping out everywhere and a background of heat blisters. She was told what had happened the night before with the centipede bite. The heat of the fire had activated the poison and intensified my reaction to it, Amma said. She called Damayanti Amma to immediately take me to the doctor. I was praying to Amma that my airway would not swell shut on the way.

Going to the doctor in those days was quite compli-cated. We set off at a brisk pace, crossing the backwater by boat, walking up the dirt road for a city block, turning right into the rice-paddy fields bordered by the backwater channels that criss-crossed everywhere in those days. It was high noon. The sun was beating down on us as we were crossing the bund separating two planted paddy sections. I was starting to feel faint, but the fear of falling from the bund into the rice paddy kept me alert. Somehow I staggered across the fields, and we made it to the doctor's house about 20 minutes later.

The doctor was elderly and intelligent-looking, with a kind, round face. Of course I did not know the Malayalam word for 'poisonous centipede bite.' But drawing with a stick in the sand would suffice. He and Damayanti Amma immediately started gravely shaking their heads in recognition of my stick drawing. The doctor disappeared into the house and emerged a moment later with three brownish yellow balls the size of a marble in the palm of his hand, a glass of water in the other. He indicated I should swallow one of the balls, and drink the water. So, I did. It was fresh and fragrant tasting, pungent actually, with a trace of bitterness. He gave the other two herb balls to Damayanti Amma and would not accept any payment. He asked me to rest on his porch lounge chair for sometime before walking back, and thankfully I sank into it. Damayanti Amma relaxed nearby to take a welcome break from the heat before walking back home.

For me, the ultimate ending to the story happened more than 20 years later. During a Tuesday Q & A program in 2009, Amma was reminiscing about the early days of the ashram. Though I had never spoken of my heat blisters to Amma, she mentioned how the ashram cook was covered with heat blisters from the cook fires, but had never offered any complaint. If we ever think Amma does not notice something, or might forget about it 20 years later, or consider it insignificant, then we are truly mistaken!

NEWS FLASH FROM THE PAST

Even more recently, more than 25 years after my days as the ashram cook, one of the original Indian householder residents stopped me while crossing in front of the Kali Temple. Pappettan Acchan wanted to show me a Malayalam circular, published as "Divya Upadesham," that he had found in a give-away pile. In it he was reading an article mentioning the ashram cook from the old days. He was remembering that was me just as I walked by! Of course he wanted to tell me what was written there.

The year was 1986, and Amma was leading an out-side program in the nearby town of Alleppy. When the program was finished Amma planned to return to the ashram with all the residents by lunch. But Amma had asked me to precede her, returning to the ashram early in order to cook for the day. However, when I arrived the cooking had already been done. So, I couldn't decide the right thing to do. Why would Amma send me back to cook if it was unnecessary? So, I decided to go ahead and light the cook fires. In the article it mentions that people began criticizing my choice, and many challenged me, saying that the food would certainly spoil and have to be thrown away, pointing out that the meal count that had been put in was a low number. But I wanted to be obedient to Amma's words. If there was too much food, it could be served in the evening. Amma would not have sent me back to cook for no reason.

It so happened that when Amma arrived back, many 'unexpected' guests had also arrived to see Amma. Only because of Amma's direction was there enough food for everyone! On the surface, Amma's words had not made sense, but the depth of her view is unerring. In the Divya Upadesha article, Amma was pointing out that the disciple will sincerely adhere to the Guru's words knowing them to contain Truth even when other people criticize them. I have yet to experience a single time when Amma's words were casual or of no consequence. When a Realized Master speaks, it is truth itself.

While I had been away in the U.S. awaiting my new visa, another Westerner had joined the ashram. She was from the Netherlands and was close to my age. We hit it off right away. Everyone loved her, and so much laughter was in the air when she was around. It so happened that a replacement was needed in the kitchen, as the Indian girl was unable to continue. When the Dutch girl was suggested to be the helper, Amma expressed a doubt that the kitchen would run smoothly with two people who were not so familiar with Indian cooking. But there were not many alternatives, and so we proceeded. At the beginning, things went alright. We loved what we were doing, but we didn't particularly know what we were doing. I remember one night, when there was so much rice left over after lunch; we came up with the idea to make rice pancakes—sort of like a potato pancake. It seemed like a good idea at the time, but try as we might, we couldn't get the pancakes to keep from falling apart on the griddle. And if the idea had worked, how would the ashram residents have felt about rice pancakes for dinner! Fortunately we still somehow managed to switch the dinner menu and finish the cooking before the bhajans ended so nobody went hungry.

BUILDING THE KALI TEMPLE

One morning a number of us were congregated in front of the meditation hall before the Upanishad class started. The big news was that the coconut trees were to be cut down to make way for a new prayer hall in the front yard. Someone offered a nostalgic feeling for the trees, but Amma wasn't having it. The trees were being sacrificed for a greater good. Currently a few people could enjoy their meditations in that spot, but this would become the place where many people would attain enlightenment and spread peace to the world. Our attachment to the trees was understandable, but we should recognize the deeper sacrifice that was to be made for the good of the world.

Once the yard was cleared, a day was carefully selected by the astrologer for maximum auspiciousness. Amma led a powerful consecration ceremony for the foundation stone that was laid into the earth. The digging of the foundation began straightaway, and materials began arriving shortly thereafter. The steel for the concrete piers, the granite rock to be smashed into small chunks for mixing in the concrete, and sacks and sacks of cement piled up along the edges of the etched-out place that marked the building's perimeter. It was a bit puzzling, the size and urgency the project, as there were still only 20 or so of us living in the ashram, but Amma insisted that we had no idea how many children would be arriving here, and we had to get a place ready for them to stay.

And so we carried sand. Tons and tons of sand, night after night, in cooking pots balanced on our heads, over the narrow footbridges that traversed the lagoon to the seaside. The sand was then compacted to fill in between the concrete footings of the foundation of the future Kali Temple. It was wonderfully hard work, full of mantra chanting to get through it, and in the wee hours of the night Amma would make hot drinks and distribute whatever snack we might have in the pantry to all of us before we turned in for a few hours of sleep.

The concrete work would sometimes fall on Bhava Darshan days. Then you would see all the devotees who had arrived, many in their best clothes, eagerly joining the tossing queue so that the *chutties* (Chinese-style steel cooking woks) full of concrete were easily moved from the concrete mixer to where the support columns were being poured. Each person would stand close to the next person so that they could toss the pan filled with concrete to their neighbor. Sometimes that involved tossing the chutties up, one by one, to the second and third stories as the younger people stood on platforms. Everyone was concentrating hard so as not to drop the concrete on the person below. There was so much good cheer and teamwork in the air on the concrete-work days, and many hungry people for lunch! In that way the Kali Temple was raised up from the ground where Amma had danced in Kali Bhava; now she was to be found throwing concrete chutties with the devotees who would attend Devi Bhava in the coming years in the temple being built by Kali herself! Once again, Amma made every task fun and manageable by her active presence on the scene. In Amma's presence, working together to get a huge project done was effortless. Even though the construction was delayed for some time in 1987 while Amma diverted resources and volunteers to take over the running of a local orphanage for 500 children that had gone bankrupt, the temple was still — amazingly — ready in time for Amma's 34th birthday celebrations in October 1987, just a little over a year after the construction began.

AMMA'S OUTSIDE PROGRAMS

It was around this same time that nearby towns and villages began inviting Amma for outside programs. Kollam,

Alleppy, Mavelikara, Harippad, Tiruvella, Kottayam, and Pandalam were some of the places I remember. A small, dark tan colored mini-bus was donated to the ashram and on the side in white letters was painted 'Mata Amritanandamayi Mission'. Six bench seats on either side of the middle aisle could seat two people comfortably, or three in a squeeze. The entire ashram could fit in the mini-bus, with Amma in the next-to-the-last seat on the right hand side. Thinking to create a bit more space for Amma, who had given so much of herself that night for the devotees I would crouch down between the bench seats, and be surprisingly comfortable. It happened many times that I could be the foot cushion for Amma's feet! An hour or two might pass in that way without my even noticing the passing time, so engrossed I was in the mood of devotion inside the mini-bus.

Thick, cream color curtains could be drawn shut and windows closed to afford privacy when we were driving through the middle of a town, causing the temperature to soar inside. Amma would laugh and say that in the ancient days the rishis would go to caves to practice austerities, but nowadays a mini-bus was enough. One of the first requirements of spiritual life is to go beyond likes and dislikes, hot and cold, pleasure and pain. If one wanted to attain liberation, one must not be adversely affected by these. Our mind should remain steady.

Amma also noticed many of us looking out at the passing view and explained, if we look outside, we never see inside. All those subtle impressions are imprinted

on the mind, even if we think we are not taking them in. Later, all those impressions will cause restless *vasanas* (tendencies) and have to be overcome. We are trying to still the thoughts of the mind when we go on pilgrimage, Amma explained, not increase the thoughts.

Depending how far we had to travel, we would leave the ashram sometime around mid-day. Stopping at the host family's house to freshen up, we would be served tea and tiffin. This was the only time we drank tea, but as it was not good for the vocal cords to drink tea before singing, generally we would decline. There were no songbooks published then, so I would hand-copy the songs Amma would sing into a diary. Often one of the residents, especially Puja Unni, who is now Swami Turiyamritananda, had been inspired to write a new song. Each song was deep in its meaning and unique in its melody. The songs were an offering of love and devotion. Amma's essential spiritual teachings could be easily understood by listening to her devotional songs.

To have mind, speech and action all dedicated to remembrance and service to God (*Manasa Vacha*), not to be a hypocrite by worshipping in the temple, but kicking the beggar at the temple gate (*Shakti Rupe*), to remember that nobody in the world is really our own (*Manase Nin Svantamayi, Bandham Illa*), to have one-pointed focus on the goal (*Adiyil Paramesvariye*), to shed innocent tears like a child before the Divine Mother for the attainment of the goal (*Ammayil Manasam*), to merge into a state of oneness with one's beloved deity through the practice of meditation and austerities (*Karuna Nir Katale*), to bathe in the inner vision of the Beloved (*Kannilenkilum*), and to attain pure and perfect peace in this world of suffering (*Ammayennulloru*). The path of love and devotion was highlighted in all of Amma's devotional songs, which we were singing at the Kalari, but also at the outside temple programs.

Amma showed me how to keep the *talam* (the beat or count of the song) by tapping one finger softly on my knee. Keeping the body still was important, the mind would get better concentration that way. Through the devotional music, the mind could be led to a point of perfect stillness. I kept trying to close the gaps between the blissful moments, as Amma had earlier advised me.

After the bhajan program, Amma would give darshan until very late. Many nights saw us piling into the mini-bus at two or three in the morning, returning to the ashram as the sun was rising. I would have a bath and then head to the kitchen, my head full of dreamy music and Amma's loving presence of the night before.

Like this, the weeks and months became a year. My practice was a blended balance of service, meditation, study of the scriptures and hatha yoga. Each one of us was following the specific guidance Amma had given, depending on whether we were more devotional or intellectual, more *tamasic* (lethargic) or *rajasic* (active) or *sattvic* (pure) in our temperament, more serene or more coarse in our bearing. Amma was the perfect reflection of what each of us held in our heart. Those full of love, reveled in love and inspiration. Those who lacked subtlety and refinement were constantly being tested. There was a noticeable difference in how Amma would instruct each one who had come to her for spiritual teaching.

As there were not many of us, it was easy to see who made time for archana and who did not. Who sat for meditation, and who had no time for it. One young woman who many years later decided to leave the ashram, rarely attended, explaining that her seva made it impossible to come. A few years later, I let my seva become an impediment to my daily practice, with disastrous effect. I mention her here and a few other times in this narrative as she had an effect on my own journey. Out of respect for her privacy, I don't include her name.

Judging others was a strong *vasana* (tendency) for me, so I tried to cultivate being the quiet observer and to work on my own self-improvement. Little did we know that Amma was purposely holding the world at bay to reserve this chance for us to grow spiritually strong before the tide came rushing in. 🪔

CHAPTER FIVE

My Children Are Crying

We were about 20 renunciates living with Amma at the Idammanel family compound in April of 1986 when Amma accepted an invitation to visit America. The invitation was from Swami Paramatmananda's brother, Earl Rosner and his wife, Judy, of America. That moment would later be remembered as a turning point for the world. At the time, I was in the midst of preparing lunch and had no clue what had just happened in the huts where Amma was meeting with some of the residents. Nealu came to the kitchen door and got my attention. He said, "Amma just accepted my brother's invitation to come to America. She sent me to ask what is needed for the trip?" I remember putting down the stirring ladle and glancing at the flames while I thought. Then I blurted out a few items off the top of my head: passports, visas, warm socks, a place for Amma to sing bhajans and posters – lots of posters would be needed because no one knew of Amma in America. When he left to go inform Amma, I thought, "What do I know about such things?" and turned back to the cooking.

Barely two hours had passed when there was a knock on the door of my hut. It was Swami Paramatmananda standing there holding a rusty typewriter. "I think you are going to need this," he said, handing it over. "Amma said you should get those things ready for the visit."

The world was going to meet Amma! She told me that afternoon, "My children are everywhere. They are crying for Amma, but cannot find me. Amma must go to them." I knew that what Amma was saying was true, as I had cried out for almost two years before hearing of Amma. There was a restlessness, a hollow ache inside that had kept me moving, urging me forward to find Amma. And surely I was not the only one out there crying in the wilderness. But how many people would have the same set of circumstances draw them out of their homes and their lives to come all this way, to the Vallikkavu jetty and across the river to meet Amma?

A DAY WITH MOTHER

My brain started shifting gears and ideas began to form. Travelling to the cities where I had friends or family seemed obvious. I would tell as many people as I could my story of meeting Amma and what was going on here. How she had healed the leper Dattan. How Amma was brilliantly guiding us on the spiritual path. Already Amma had started one school, and a free one-room health clinic where a doctor and nurse provided primary care and medicine to the poor villagers from the island. I sat with Swami Paramatmananda to share my thoughts and pick his brain. We decided to film a short documentary about life with Amma. We named it "A Day with Mother." Amma gave her blessing for the filming and Swami Paramatmananda worked day and night to get it ready in time for my departure. We did a shorter one called, "Amrita Sagara: Ocean of Bliss" based on Amma's teachings. Saumya (now Swamini Krishnamrita) did the sound track. We figured these films would be the best way to introduce Amma to as many people as I could.

Swami Paramatmananda's mom was in Chicago; my family was in Pittsburgh and Boston. His first yoga teacher was in Madison. His brother and all my college friends, in the Bay Area. Those would be places I could go easily, though at the time I had no idea how to travel around, as I had no money to do any of this. We both started writing letters. One day an aerogram arrived at the ashram. It was from a man by the name of George Brunswig, writing from San Francisco. He had heard about a booklet titled "The Mother of Sweet Bliss," describing the life of an Indian saint named Amma. Could we please send him the booklet, and he would reimburse the cost and shipping? He was our first outside contact! I wrote back to him the same day. Explained I would be coming to the Bay Area and would have copies of the booklet with me. I would call him sometime in the early summer, if that was alright.

ROUND TRIP BECOMES AROUND THE WORLD

The most amazing thing happened when I went to the travel agency in Kochi. After explaining to the agent what I needed, a basic roundtrip ticket to San Francisco and back two months later, we got to talking as she looked up fares. I shared a little bit of what I was doing, not thinking that she would be very interested. But she got this funny look on her face and told me about a great deal. For only a little bit more money, I could pick two airlines and 10 cities. Get an around-the-world ticket and have 10 stops total?! For only $1,000?! I almost fell off my chair. That was exactly what was needed! My next thought was that meant Europe could easily be included. It seemed an auspicious start. In my mind, Amma's trip to America was transformed into a world tour in the space of a moment. I told the travel agent I would be in touch in the next few days. Returning to the ashram I couldn't wait to tell Amma of this great, new development.

Amma didn't bat an eyelash. She was gardening when I told her. She just looked up and said, "OK, daughter, whatever you think is best. One of Amma's children is in France, and you can write to him. See what he thinks," and went back to her gardening. Amma is the most detached person I have ever met. I might have elicited more response had I come up with a good way to use up leftover rice.

GIFTS THAT GIVE

Before my departure, I went to seek Amma's blessings. She gave me two parting gifts. The first was a simple, medium-sized, brass oil lamp. I should light the lamp before each video show on a side table. Smiling a twinkling smile, Amma pointed to the top piece of the lamp and said, "third eye," marking it with *kumkum* (a red powder sacred to the Divine Mother), then pointed to the bottom piece and said "feet," pointing to two spots on the rim, and marking them as well. I could imagine the Divine Mother sitting there, keeping me company.

The second gift was a ring. Amma had gotten out a small jewelry box and set it beside her while we were talking. Opening it she handed over a silver ring with an inlaid enamel portrait of her with a sky-blue background. She wanted me to have it. I was so touched that tears sprang to my eyes. Trying it on immediately, it fit perfectly on my left-hand index finger. That ring was my solace for the many, many miles which would be covered before Amma and I were reunited later that summer. Amma then told me, "Daughter, never ask for anything and everything will come to you." Years later, when reading the Ramayana for the first time, I could understand why Rama gave Hanuman the ring to verify Rama's identity to his beloved Sita Devi. While I am no Hanuman, Amma's *sankalpa* (divine intention) would have been felt by her children in foreign lands through the presence of the ring which I wore. With absolute faith in Amma's words, I moved forward in an eastward direction around the world.

ON THE ROAD

When I set off on my trip in June of 1986, I had no idea that it would actually be but the first of three such trips back and forth across the United States and across Europe

for me. Amma would only begin her World Tour a year later. Before then, thousands of miles would turn into tens of thousands of miles of effort to bring Amma to the West for her children who were crying. I had no plan to follow, no devotees to contact. No book, "Planning World Tours for Dummies" to serve as my guide. My family had simply bought me a ticket to visit them and I set out. Little did they know what a whirlwind visit it would be, and that in less than a year an Indian saint named Amma would stay in their own house!

Landing in San Francisco with a backpack containing one change of clothes, the brass oil lamp, copies of the booklet "The Mother of Sweet Bliss," and the two videos we had produced, I set off across the country and around the world, showing the video to as many people as possible in every city where there was family or friend. In those places I could always count on food and shelter, loving kindness and generosity of spirit. Each time when ideas ran out, or it seemed the trail had gone cold, Amma's grace would lead me in the next direction. As there was no possibility to call Amma, by necessity I had to listen with my heart for what Amma wanted. Those meditations led in every direction imaginable.

THE FIRST VIDEO SHOWING

The very first public video showing of "A Day With Mother" took place in San Francisco and was arranged by George Brunswig, the man from San Francisco who had sent the aerogram request for "The Mother of Sweet Bliss" booklet. It was attended by nearly two dozen people. During the question-and-answer session afterwards, it was obvious that a number of them had connected with Amma during the video. As the group headed to the living room for refreshments, two people approached me, introducing themselves as Tina and Nancy. If there was anything they could do, they would love to help. I felt Amma had sent two angels without delay. We arranged a time to meet again and they gave directions to Berkeley where they lived.

HOW CAN WE HELP?

A few days later, as I headed to the appointment with Tina and Nancy, I was wondering how it would go. What was the next step? Ask for nothing and everything would come, that had been Amma's mandate. It certainly kept things simple! As it turned out, Tina was the mother of an adorable seven year old boy, Theo. Nancy was a research scientist at UC Berkeley. They wanted to hear more Amma stories and ask questions, and we talked for more than two hours. As I took leave, they again expressed their keen desire to help me in any way possible. Since very few people knew of Amma in the US, I felt it would be a good idea to work with them. I hadn't asked; they had offered. They fit the criteria!

They began by arranging more video showings that led me to make more and more contacts. One person was going to Mount Shasta, someone else knew a family in Miranda. In this way, I let go and let happen. With few exceptions, scenes like this unfolded in each city and town I stopped in across the US, regardless of how many had attended the video showing. One or two, sometimes three people would come forward and express more interest. Following up with those two or three people in each town, and engaging them in the process of planning is what made it all work. Each one in their own way ended up making such sincere effort on behalf of the first world tour, long before they met Amma, just on the basis of having seen "A Day With Mother." I took it as a sign of Amma's pure grace that every necessary detail manifested at the right moment.

WHAT'S IN A NAME?

George Brunswig had offered to help me make a pamphlet about Amma's life. We sat for hours working on the layout. I had already written a summary of Amma's life and her teachings to appear on the inside panels, and the back panel was set aside to announce the tour. I had this idea that by writing it down, it helped to bring the concept of the tour into creation. The back caption under a favorite picture of Amma read:

"Dates and Places of Amma's Visit" and then went on to list San Francisco, Seattle, Mt. Shasta, Big Sur, Santa Cruz, the Southwest, Chicago, Madison, Pittsburgh, Boston and New York City.

That same day we had a conversation about getting a post office box so that we would have a mailing address, and for that we needed a name. Getting a name felt important, it made things more real by my way of thinking. So we went back and forth about it, George and I. Amma's ashram in India at that time was called Mata Amritanandamayi Mission or MA Mission. George didn't think that would work in America, as "Mission" was typically a Christian designation. I suggested Mata Amritanandamayi Centre, or MA Centre. I liked the British spelling of Centre, and George did not. He said that it was always a good idea to stick to spelling things the way they were spelled in the country you were in – so it should be M.A. Center. I had to agree with his logic, and so, in the span of a 10 minute conversation, M.A. Center came into being. It could only be Amma's grace that a simple moment of writing down "M.A. Center" would attain such longevity and become home to so much selfless service.

COMPASS POINTS

North, south, east, west; by bus, by car, by plane, by train. Sleeping in family's and friends' homes, apartments, tepees and even the occasional yurt, my intention was to show the "Day with Mother" video as many times as I possibly could in those two months. Whether it was for one person or a circle of 25, I would follow the same format: light the lamp, tell about Amma's life, and show the video. Afterwards I would talk about the time I had spent with Amma and answer questions until each person was satisfied. Explaining that Amma would be coming next summer and if anyone wished to stay in touch as the tour plans came together, I asked people to write their name and address in my notebook. Those names eventually became the core group across America that would host Amma. Sometimes people had brought food for a potluck and we would stay up late talking about spiritual life with Amma. It was always evident who had made a connection with Amma during the evening presentation. From this network of people sprang new connections, more video showings, more contact between Amma and Her children, all of it directed by Amma's unfailing grace.

By mid-August, having travelled for more than 60 days without pause, I thankfully returned to Amma's side, having visited Singapore, San Francisco, Oakland, Berkeley, Carmel, Santa Cruz, Mt. Shasta, Miranda, Seattle, Olympia, Taos, Santa Fe, Albuquerque, Boulder, Madison, Chicago, Pittsburgh, Baltimore, Washington DC, New York, Boston, London, Zurich, Schweibenalpe, and Graz.

RETURNING HOME

Amma was sitting on the front porch of the Kalari that day in August of 1986 when I returned to the ashram. Some of the residents had also joined Amma there and were curious to know how my time had been spent. What was happening? When would Amma be leaving for America?

Where were the places Amma would be visiting? How many people had heard of Amma? I recall the volley of questions being both exciting and overwhelming, and I struggled to answer them in a clear way. Then I looked over at Amma. She was completely quiet, seeming to be taking it all in. Then, she looked up and her deep eternal eyes locked on to mine, and there was stillness in the air.

"*Sheriyayo, mole?*" was all Amma asked me. (Is it all okay, daughter?) The effect that Amma's simple and direct question had on me can't be described. It was as if the air itself had stopped breathing, waiting for my answer. Time was momentarily suspended while Amma tested my heart's ability to carry her message to the faraway children and bring Amma to them, all the while being far away from Amma's physical presence in order to do so. Intuitively I sensed that Amma was measuring my resolve. Calmly and deliberately I replied, "*Sheriyayi*, Amme." (All is okay, Amma.) And in that moment I felt a surge of energy in my chest, as if a subtle bridge of divine love was connecting Amma's heart and my own. Amma smiled compassionately at me and held me in her arms for a long time. Amma wanted me to go and rest from the journey. When I stood up to take leave of Amma, I could unmistakably sense a deep bond had been sealed between us that would give me "all that was needed without my asking." In that moment my soul knew that the tour was on, that Amma would be with her children around the world before long. At the same time I sensed that a lot of effort and sacrifice would go into it. I remember a tremendous feeling of joy spreading over me.

There was not a moment to waste. The next day I proposed that a newsletter be started to send to the people on the mailing list I had collected. "What? A newsletter? But Amma hasn't even visited the US yet," was the general response. Not satisfied, I went to ask Amma about my idea. She heartily agreed, asking me to bring a tape recorder and a set of questions from my time away. She would answer questions for the first issue. Not only that, but with her own hand She wrote a letter to send to all those who had signed onto the mailing list. I proposed to name the newsletter "Amritanandam," Immortal Bliss, after Amma's own name.

BUYING THE PLANE TICKETS

The plane ticket I had traveled on during the summer was a dream ticket. It had worked very well for the initial tour planning, and my idea was to get the same ticket for Amma and the group. There was only one problem: there was no money to purchase the tickets. This was very much in the back of my mind as the weeks and months passed.

Even before coming to Amma, I had always been a very frugal person. I didn't have a credit card in my name and had never owned a car which, for an American girl, was uncommon. The only impulsive thing I had done my whole life was to travel to India to meet Amma. Now that I was living at the ashram, the only back-up I had in

case of emergency was an American Express credit card
my parents had given me on the condition it would be
used only if absolutely necessary.

Everything would come that was needed; Amma had
been clear about that. The plane fare for the tour would be
no exception, I was absolutely certain. It was just a matter of timing. But this particular need was pressing—the
plane tickets were needed to apply for the US visas. The
French visas could be obtained on the weight of the US
visas. Only then could the more detailed planning proceed. Only then would the dream of bringing Amma to
her children take one more critical step in the direction
of becoming a reality.

The recollection of Amma's words, "My children are
crying for me, they are unable to find me," spurred me
onward. I myself had cried for two years before meeting
Amma and knew what that felt like. More than anything,
I wanted Amma and her children to be reunited the way
I had been reunited with her. Amma's longing to see her
children had become my longing to see Amma with her
children. I decided some risk would have to be taken; we
had to proceed.

I broached the subject with Swami Paramatmananda.
I knew that he had the same arrangement with his mom
as I did with mine — the in-case-of-emergency card! My
practical suggestion to him was that we go to the travel
agent in Kochi and split the tickets down the middle – I
would buy five, and he would buy five. I assured him that

the money would come; I had complete faith in that. If not, I solemnly swore to get a job cooking at the end of the tour to repay the debt. Without hesitation he agreed that was a sound solution. We left for Kochi within the hour, not breathing a word of our plan to anyone.

The two airlines were Singapore Air and Delta; the 10 cities were Singapore, San Francisco, Albuquerque, Chicago, Washington DC, Boston, New York, Paris, Zurich and Vienna. As the sound of the travel agent passing our credit cards through the old-fashioned machine clicked away 10 times, in my heart I knew the tour was on.

THE US CONSULATE-CHENNAI

The task that would absorb my attention for nearly three months was applying for all the passports, procuring the US & French visas and getting the plane tickets for Amma and the nine others who would go on tour. The passports were easy, but the visas were another matter. In those days, even for a short visit, American sponsors were required for Amma and the monks. It was very difficult to get one visa, much less seven of them. In fact, although none of the families I approached for sponsorship had met Amma, they were all ready to sponsor Amma's group.

A feeling of trepidation was weighing heavily on me as I waited in the Kayamkulam bus station for the 17-hour bus ride to take me to the US Consulate in Chennai. I had no appointment, no plan in particular as to how to get the visas, no agent in tow to make our case. The bit of research I had been able to do indicated only that it was unheard of to get what we needed without many months of waiting. If we were declined, we had to wait a year before re-applying. I knew the determining factor, as always, would be Amma's prevailing grace. One of Amma's countless miracles was to arrange all such matters without the slightest hitch. But still, the effort had to be made. With the set of 10 plane tickets, passports and seven sponsorship letters safely tucked in my backpack, I boarded the bus, spending most of the time praying not to return empty-handed and nibbling on peanut brittle. If the visas were not granted, it would leave the tour plans in tatters, at least for the timetable that I had carefully laid out.

Walking into the consulate, I found myself amidst dozens and dozens of people waiting in the entry hall, some pacing around and each one holding a large number tag waiting to be called over to a glassed-in area where the clerks were seated. Scanning the noisy, nervous crowd, I felt the air go still again, just as it had on the porch of the Kalari with Amma some months before. I decided to forgo the number system and walked right up to the glass window to get a clerk's attention. In quiet tones I leaned forward and explained what was needed… seven visas to visit America for two months this summer. No, none of the applicants were married. No, not even engaged. No, none of them owned businesses. But, yes, all of them would be certain to return to India in August. Yes, I did know they would need sponsors. I held up the sponsorship packet nodding 'yes.' I smiled shakily at the clerk while internally reciting Amma's words, "Ask for nothing, and all will come... Ask for nothing, all will come..." The clerk swung open the door and ushered me into one of the offices for the interview.

I heard myself explaining what was needed, and watched in stunned silence the hand stamping over and over again, the visas into all the passports. As it turned out, less than one hour was spent getting all the visas issued; tears of gratitude poured down my cheeks standing outside on the sidewalk. That same afternoon I caught the first in a series of buses that would deliver me back home. One more follow-up trip to Pondicherry was needed to secure the French visas which also proceeded smoothly.

READY, SET, GO!

It is hard to imagine those days when there was no computer, no cell phone and no internet, but all the planning for the first tour took place without any of that. The small typewriter that had been given to me was my way to contact people, to type up the "Amritanandam" newsletter and to keep in touch with the small and scattered group of people who had been eager to help after seeing the video of Amma in the summer. The Europe tour planning had been given over to a devotee living in France, Jacques Albohair. He would follow up there with the contacts I had made, adding to those he already had, while I figured out Amma's tour in America.

By January I knew that it was time to return to America. Now that we had the plane tickets and the visas had been granted, the substance of the tour was what was needed. Where would Amma and the group stay? Which exact cities and towns would Amma visit? What halls would be suitable for the evening bhajans and darshan? How about all those publicity posters that needed to be put up everywhere? Who would be there to do all that? I decided to cross the country again, even though it would be the dead of winter. More video showings would mean more contacts, more helpers, and more of Amma's children would come to hear of Amma's upcoming visit. It was the only way I could see to move forward. So, starting in San Francisco I would not stop until I reached Boston. Asking for Amma's blessing, my ticket for the US was booked for February 3rd.

GETTING MY N.O.R. VISA

One small detail I had pushed to the back of my mind was my own visa. I would need a No Objection to Return (N.O.R.) visa to get back into India at the end of the tour. I had received my visa extension the previous year, but now I had to go out of the country again to continue Amma's tour planning. It had been hard enough to convince the Foreigner's Registration Office in Kollam that I had to go out of the country last August, how would they treat this second request for a N.O.R. visa, less than six months later? They didn't like it, but they accepted my application.

The real problem came when the police arrived at the ashram to do the routine inquiry to process my N.O.R. request. I was summoned to the office in Amma's family house. Two police inspectors had come and they wanted to see my passport, my residential permit and to speak with me. As the three of us took our seats in the tiny office, a feeling of claustrophobia came over me.

First the police wanted to know why I had to go out of India again. I was here on an entry visa, they told me, and it was not possible to come and go so frequently, two times in less than a year. What was my explanation? I mentioned my family needing to see me, and told them that some other things needed my attention. They were not at all satisfied with that answer. They gave me an ultimatum: either stay put and keep my long-term visa, or go out of the country and forfeit my entry visa. The visa that I had waited so long for — the visa that made it possible for me not to have to leave Amma every six months!

For a moment, my mind raced back and forth between the two possibilities, but there was really no choice. If I opted for keeping my entry visa, the tour planning would come to a grinding halt. That was no longer an option in my mind; the planning was too far along. I could not accept those terms; I told the police that I had to go to the US, so I would sacrifice my long-term visa. Without another word, they wrote on the back of my registration papers, "Permission to leave: granted, permission to return: denied," rendering the visa null and void. My heart was thudding in my chest as we stood up to leave. That was it; my precious visa was gone with the stroke of a pen. There was no point in thinking about it, there was nothing more to be done. I didn't feel to tell anyone the bad news; it could wait for later.

MANTRA DIKSHA IN THE KALARI

The time to leave for the second round of organizing in the US was fast approaching. Amma had indicated that I would be given *mantra diksha* (a formal initiation into the practice of mantra) in the Kalari before my departure. This was a moment I had been preparing for since joining the Ashram in 1983. I had observed the transformative effect the initiation had on the few other residents who had received *diksha* in the privacy of the Kalari and hoped that I would be a fit recipient for Amma's grace. It is said that the Guru transmits a portion of their own vital, awakened energy during the initiation as a means to hasten the student's process of awakening.

Two days before, I was told that this coming Sunday would be the day of my initiation. I began my fast, although I did take light food in the evening to keep my strength up. Late Sunday afternoon before Devi Bhava I took a bath and changed into a brand-new set of clothes. I sat for meditation inside the Kalari. As Bhava Darshan continued into the night, the feeling of anticipation heightened. It was an unusually big crowd, and Amma only finished around 3:30 in the morning. The temple doors were closed and I remained inside with Amma, who was still in her silk Devi Bhava sari. Dr. Leela, who is now known as Swamini Atmaprana, was also there to attend to Amma during my initiation.

Amma began by seating me on the same foot stool that she had just used during the Devi Bhava. Then she moved to the altar behind the peetham. Folding my legs into the full lotus position, my back lightly touching the front of the peetham, I was facing east, towards the closed temple doors. The bhajan music was continuing out on the front porch, the monks singing beautiful songs to Devi, the Divine Mother. I turned my attention inward, away from the music. My gaze was averted downward, and I could hear Amma chanting some of the powerful, ancient hymns of Devi I had heard when consecration ceremonies were being conducted. I felt completely relaxed and receptive in that moment.

Then Amma came forward carrying a red hibiscus flower garland. She garlanded me and placed fresh sandalwood paste on my forehead. She held her index finger on my third eye for a long time. I focused my mind on the syllable 'ma' and held it in that one-pointed awareness, streaming my thoughts into the image of my *ishta devata*, the Divine Mother. Amma continued her chanting, but in deeper, softer tones. It was effortless to let my mind surrender. There was no thought, no temple, no time — only a feeling of complete oneness. After how long I don't know, Amma was whispering a mantra in my right ear, her finger closing off the other ear, as if to prevent what she was uttering from passing out the other side. Three times she repeated the mantra and then moved away, behind me to the altar. I could hear the rustling of her heavy silk sari and the jingling of her anklets dancing in time with the bhajans; it was indescribably beautiful. Amma had begun to dance; Swamini Atmaprana told me this the next morning. Tears were streaming down my face without any particular emotion associated with them. More time passed. With the mantra echoing inside, the *mantra shakti* (the power of the mantra) reverberating in every cell of my body, I stayed in that suspended state of meditative consciousness.

The initiate could stay inside the temple for as long as they needed after Amma had gone out. The first rays of sunrise caressed my face as I silently emerged from the Kalari and returned to my hut.

PERMISSION FOR A PRE-TOUR

A day later, while packing to go, an idea popped into my head. Why not put together a 'pre-tour' with a few of the monks sent ahead to precede Amma? We could travel to each place Amma would visit, present an evening of *satsang* (spiritual discourse) and sing *bhajans*. Then, after the video showing, they could share their much vaster experience of Amma with the people. Plus, all the halls and homes I was planning to arrange this coming month could be checked out to make sure everything was suitable. Even though I knew it would add a layer of complexity to plan a pre-tour while at the same time planning for Amma's visit, I decided to ask Amma about it. No one really much liked the idea except Amma. She smiled so sweetly when I told her my idea for the pre-tour, and she picked which monks would travel to the US in advance of Amma.

The pre-tour date was fixed for March 26th. The monks would fly into San Francisco, bringing the harmonium and a tabla set, and we would drive across the country. Swami Amritaswarupananda began composing beautiful *Hari Kathas* ("The Story of the Lord," set to music). One would be on Amma's life story; the other one about Meerabhai, the 14th century saint. These he planned to share during the pre-tour programs. With all that in place, I set off.

EMERGENCE OF THE DIVINE WEB

Crossing the US that winter was extremely cold, but every day I managed one video showing and at least one decent meal. Sometimes a contact from the summer would arrange for me to show a video, other times I would simply walk into a bookstore and see who might want to watch Amma's video. I was not fussy; Amma's children were everywhere and she was my guiding light. Poring over the Yellow Pages phone book, I would arrange to meet informally with members of different church denominations and spiritual centers to speak of Amma. Many decided to host an evening program in their church or meeting hall

free-of-charge: the Quakers, the Unitarians, the Vipas-
sana Meditation Center, the Cambridge Zen Center,
the Theosophical Society, the Sufis, the Yoga Society,
the Ramalayam Temple in Chicago, St. John the Divine
Church in New York City, even Harvard University were
all interested. The tour was shaping up; the details were
coming into focus.

In the cities where I had made contacts the summer
before, we would all meet to look for venues and come
up with a publicity plan and start making lists. We were
constantly talking about Amma and the pre-tour. Everyone could feel the excitement building. We were getting
to know each other by working together on a common
goal, to bring Amma into our midst. Their innocent faith
in doing this selfless service, having never met Amma,
was blossoming. It was totally inspiring to watch and
be a part of. Their inner compass was guiding them in
Amma's direction. Clearly these were Amma's children
and it was with great anticipation that I looked forward
to being there for their first darshans.

As the planning solidified, one of the first questions
I had to tackle was where exactly Amma would go. No
one knew Amma. The only invitation we had was to the
Bay Area. But I didn't see that as an obstacle. I always
imagined Amma blowing on a dandelion, the airborne
seeds landing where my family and friends lived. These
became the central cities Amma would visit, scattered
across the country. But these seeds in turn germinated,

having been sprinkled with the water of Amma's pure grace, and like tendrils growing from a creeper, the other locations emerged.

From the first video showing in San Francisco came invitations to visit Mt. Shasta, which in turn led me to Miranda, to Seattle. Then Carmel and Santa Cruz. Taos, New Mexico was full of old friends and spiritual seekers eager to meet Amma as that was where I was living when I heard about Amma. From there came Santa Fe, Albuquerque, and Lama Mountain. Nealu's mother, Phyllis Rosner was in Chicago. His first yoga teacher was in Madison. My father was living in Boston. I really wanted Amma to visit New York and Washington DC. I felt Amma must do programs in these cities, as so many powerful, far-reaching decisions were made in them. Amma's divine energy could definitely be beneficial in them. However we did not know anyone who lived in either place. Thus I had to start from scratch. In this way, I zigged and zagged across the country. Amma was constantly arranging connections between people and cities; all there was for me to do was see the thread and follow it. Families began offering to have Amma stay in their homes. Even after explaining it would not just be Amma, but rather all 10 of us, they were still very welcoming, without exception. Doors were opening everywhere. In this way, what had seemed like a huge, impersonal country just two months before became an interconnected web of divine potential — a pattern was emerging.

WITH ONLY FIVE DOLLARS IN MY POCKET

Often it was the case where there was only five dollars in my pocket, but somehow Amma always made sure that I was getting by. An old friend from college would drive me more than a thousand miles to Taos, or someone from a video showing would offer a Greyhound bus ticket for me to get to the next place. Hundreds and then thousands of miles passed by in those six weeks; it was me, my backpack and an intense longing to bring Amma to Her children.

On March 20th I had arrived in New York City. Whew! In one week the monks would arrive in San Francisco and we would begin the pre-tour. My family in Boston had generously offered to fly me back in time to meet them on the 26th. The overall feeling was that everything was progressing well. Yet I must admit to a nagging concern. My hope had been that there would be more financial security by this point. As of now, nothing more than enough to get me to the next town had materialized. However I had to keep going; the planning was too far along to let this nagging worry stand in my way.

The more pressing problem was that I didn't have a way to get to Boston. I was staying in New York City with a childhood friend of my mother, Ann Wyma, who taught theater at NYU. She had kindly arranged a video showing that night on campus. I was pretty sure it would be a good turn-out and that someone I had yet to meet might have a ride for me to Boston. It had happened that way before.

Can you imagine my disappointment when I arrived to do the video showing and only one person turned up? And he had only showed up because he had thought it was a video about the martial arts of Kerala. He felt so sorry for me that he stayed while I lit the oil lamp and spoke of Amma and the upcoming tour. Needless to say, he was not heading to Boston.

It got worse. When I came out of the hall, it had started snowing heavily. There were 20 blocks to walk as I didn't even have bus fare. Buttoning up my jacket, my head facing into the biting wind, I began trudging back. Without mercy the snowfall thickened as blizzard-like conditions set in. Finally and all at once, it was too much for me. I stopped in the middle of the sidewalk and peered up into sky; a feeling of utter despair overwhelmed me. All I could hear in the whistling wind were the words that Amma had spoken so many months before. "Ask for nothing and everything you need will come to you, darling daughter."

Hot tears spilled onto my cheeks, and I felt my knees giving way as I knelt, in the snow, on the sidewalk, on that New York City night. People pushed past me, jostling me, in their hurry to get out from the storm. And there I prayed. I poured my entire being into that prayer. It was a rescue call to Amma to please hear me and to show Her hand, to reach me in this desolate, forlorn condition and to let me know I was reaching Her. It was my moment of greatest need. Why were my hands empty, Amma? Why did 3,000 miles separate me from where I needed to be? How could I hope to proceed? How would I welcome the monks in one week when I couldn't even get myself to Boston the next day? Was there something lacking on my part? Was there some other sacrifice more to be made?

After that, I don't remember much about walking the 20 blocks, except that it was very, very cold. The next morning I woke up to an empty apartment. In a rather dismal mood I went into the kitchen where there was a note on the countertop. It read:

Dear Gretchen,

I don't know what your project is, but I wanted to help you...Ann

And she had left me three $20 bills. I knew the bus fare to Boston was $58. My throat tightened, Amma had come through once again.

But the best was yet to come. When I arrived at my Dad's house in Boston later that day, he told me that two different families had been trying to reach me. They had called that morning hoping to locate me and he handed me their phone numbers. I called them. Both families said the same thing: they couldn't stop thinking about Amma since seeing her in the video some weeks before. The night before, they had felt an urge to try and track me down. They wanted to contribute some money to help make the tour happen- with the pre-tour coming up and Amma arriving in eight weeks, surely I must be in need of something. And they both contributed exactly $5,000!

The sun had not yet had a chance to set even once since I had offered my prayer to Amma. Not one, but two of her hands she had shown. This is the pure grace who is Amma.

CHAPTER SIX

Sweeping The Path

April 1987
Oakland, California

As the invitation for Amma to visit the United States
had come from Swami Paramatmananda's brother's
family, the Rosners, it was there I picked up the monks
for the pre-tour. The Rosner residence, in a suburb of
Oakland, had become home base; their generosity was a
welcome and constant beacon throughout the organizing
for Amma's first world tour.

Having just returned from Boston, I was scampering
about, going over lists with Judy Rosner — lists of food
and spices we needed, another list of warm clothes we
needed, with everyone's sizes. A 'checklist of readiness' for
each of the 15 cities and towns Amma would visit, covering
everything from airport pick-up to yurt cleaning supplies.
Then another list for the pre-tour stops — everything
from cooking pots, to the brass puja articles that would
be needed to welcome Amma. A master list of current
contacts — new leads, suggestions, and requests. The list
of air tickets and flight timings. Before long, I needed a
list of lists, just to keep them straight.

Watching me from the kitchen table, Earl Rosner said, "Kusuma, slow down, sit on the sofa and relax. Amma is coming, everything will be fine. Don't spoil the sweetness of Amma by dragging her around to so many places." My reaction was immediate. I suppose I was tired. "Amma's sweetness is fixed; it can never change. We already have Amma in our life. She's coming to see her new children. She's not traveling all this way for us. Amma's sweetness is in the embrace of her children, so there is only more and more sweetness to look forward to. It's one of Amma's greatest joys to light the lamp of love in someone's heart. Please don't say that to me again." I was at once dismayed by the sharp answer that had tumbled out, but Earl only laughed as a big brother would, and said he admired my determination, and conceded that maybe he should be the one to sit down on the sofa!

Although my first two organizing laps across the US had already exceeded 10,000 miles, I felt as fresh as a daisy as I drove to the airport the morning of March 26th. A tight-knit circle of Bay Area spiritual seekers had been working diligently to pull off our next 6,000 miles, the Pre-Tour, as we called it. They made pamphlets, hosted more video showings, reached out to friends and family along the route, donated their vehicles, bought warm socks and bedding, prepared yummy vegetarian food, cleaned house, and spent hours putting up with me and my lists!

The pre-tour would set out on April 1st, in an old but sturdy Dodge van loaned to us by Jack Dawson, an old friend of the Rosner family. I would drive the monks across the country and back again as they held satsang and bhajan programs in every city and town where Amma would be going in May, June and July. My hope was that more people would hear about Amma's upcoming tour, and that the program venues that had been arranged could be checked out. I wanted to eliminate any unpleasant surprises now, not when Amma was touring. The pre-tour was a dry run of sorts. I had allotted six weeks for it.

Larry Kelley, a native of San Francisco who had attended the very first video show, and I shared the driving as we headed 1,000 miles north for Seattle on the first leg of the journey. We travelled first to Mount Shasta, where Swami Amritaswarupananda threw his first snowball and the monks slept in their first yurt. Then we went to Miranda, where they encountered their first majestic Redwood trees. Scott Stevens, an old friend from New Mexico, would replace Larry as my co-pilot for all points east, and after another 2,000 miles, we picked him up at a mid-way point in Carson, New Mexico.

For meals, I would cook kitcheri on a small camp stove. Warm cocoa and tea on the same stove would keep us in a bit of comfort. At the host homes where we would stay, the monks had their first contact with a completely different culture. The potluck receptions were the first of many food explorations they would encounter. Swami Amritaswarupananda encountered his first distasteful plate of "grass," a.k.a. salad. The monks encountered

the enthusiastic American "bear hugs" of greeting, which I quickly learned to tactfully deflect for them. "We are monks, Kusuma. Can you please head them off at the pass?" Each monk was gifted with a new Coleman sleeping bag, which became a best friend of sorts as we made our way through some chilly weather crossing the Rocky Mountains in early spring. The scenery we were passing must have looked like we were in another world! I can't imagine how much they were longing for Amma.

Writing for *"Amritanandam"* in the March 1987 issue, Swami Paramatmananda wrote:

Dear Brothers and Sisters,

....We arrived on 26th March at my brother, Earl Rosner's, house, the person who invited Holy Mother to America. Since that time we have been travelling with Kusuma and Mr. Larry Kelly in California, Oregon and Washington, going to the places where Mother will be visiting, making arrangements for her programmes and also doing bhajan and meeting with the devotees. The response has been very good and devotees everywhere are eagerly looking forward to having Mother's Darshan next month. We are feeling Mother's Divine Hand at every step and are surprised to hear the stories narrated by devotees here of their experiences gained through Amma's Grace. Though Amma's physical form is 12,000 miles away in India, Her all-pervading Self does not seem to be limited by time and space as she blesses Her children all over the world!

Kusuma is engaged in driving us thousands of miles all over the United States, arranging all of Mother's and our programs, cooking for us and just generally acting as a small mother looking after us in all ways. Because of all these activities she has been unable to find any time this month to write in the newsletter and that is why Nealu is sitting at the typewriter now between two halts.

In Amma,

Br.Nealu (Swami Paramatmananda)

The monks' presence was remarkable and spoke volumes to Amma's greatness. Swami Amritaswarupananda performed the *Hari Kathas* he had composed, creating a mood of sublime devotion as we made our way from town to town. Swami Paramatmananda, originally from the U.S., began giving inspiring talks before each showing of "A Day With Mother." We were singing our hearts out for Amma, without any microphones, and her divine presence came through so powerfully. They led unbelievably transformative programs. "Prabhu Misham" was one of the 1987 pre-tour bhajans that really got to people; "Gajanana" and "Kaya Pia," "Gopala Krishna" and "Karunalaye Devi," "Narayana Hari" and "Gangadhara Hara" were others. The Q&A sessions following the video were lively and insightful. What had been a mere dozen people at my video showing just a month before doubled into an attendance of 25-30 strong throughout the pre-tour. More and more Amma tour posters and pamphlets were distributed along the way.

Another 1,500 miles and we had reached Madison. And there on the green grass of the Lawrence family farm, our borrowed, trusty Dodge van breathed its last. It was a solemn moment, and the monks performed a closing puja for its heroic selfless service. It had transported and sheltered us these past 4,000 miles, never once leaving us stranded along a lonely stretch of highway. Jack took the news well. But I had to come up with a plan quickly, as we were only halfway through the pre-tour and the clock was ticking. Bus tickets to Chicago, a cheap flight to New York, a train ride along the eastern seaboard to touch base with Washington DC and Boston. We would have to fly back to San Francisco; there was no way around it. My head and heart were spinning with the effort to hold the focus, stay grounded and keep the pace steady. By the time we reached Boston, Amma would be arriving on the West Coast in less than 10 days.

Recently, reminiscing about the pre-tour with Swami Amritaswarupananda and Swami Paramatmananda, we were hard pressed to recall any hardship at all, though the road trip was grueling. We had laughed and cried count-less times along the way, and shared profound moments of Amma's presence and pure grace that humbled us and brought tears to our eyes. For each one of us, it represented a maturing phase of our spiritual life. We were engaged in a process of bringing Amma to the world, a huge turning point, and we wanted to do it in the best way possible. Our effort was our offering, her grace was pouring down on us from all sides. It was only years later that I came to know that it was very unusual for disciples to precede their Guru in such a manner, but as I didn't know any better, with Amma's blessing, we did what was needed to be done to spread the word of Amma's first world tour.

Remembering the core group, primarily from the first video showing of "A Day With Mother" in San Francisco, without whom I would not be writing this chapter: George Brunswig, Tina Hari Sudha Jencks, the late Nancy Crawford (Brahmacharini Nirmalamrita), the late Larry Kelley, Susan Rajita Cappadocia, Robin Ramani Cohelan, James Mermer, Cherie McCoy, Jack Dawson, Timothy Conway, Michael Hock, Scott Stevens, Candice Sarojana Strand, my sister Katherine Ulrich and, of course, Earl and Judy Rosner. This group was in from the beginning, making real sacrifices to help bring Amma to the West, and additionally honored to be the welcoming committee for the monks who conducted the pre-tour.

The families who hosted Amma and the pre-tour were the Rosners, living in Oakland; the family of the late Marion Rosen – Tina & Theo Jencks of Berkeley; Ron Gottsegen of Carmel and Sandhya Kolar of Carmel, the Iyer family of Palo Alto; Liesbeth and Ivo Obregon of Santa Cruz; the late Elizabeth Wagner of Weed; Susan Rajita Cappadocia of Mount Shasta; Ken and Judy Goldman of Miranda; Terri Hoffman's family of Seattle; the late Feeny Lipscomb and Bruce Ross of Taos; Isabella Raiser and Bob Draper of Taos; the Schmidt family of Santa Fe; the Pillai family of Albuquerque; Balachandran and Lakshmi Nair of Chicago; the late Phyllis Rosner of Chicago; Barbara, David and Rasya Lawrence of Madison; Mary La Mar and Michael Price also of Madison; Phyllis Sujata Castle of New York; Gena Glicklich of Boston; the late Mirabhai of the Washington DC area; Kit Simms of Maryland; the Devan family of Connecticut; the McGregor family of Pittsburgh; and the folks of Plain Pond Farm.

Amma beautifully arranged everything, as always, once my effort was fully expended. More and more people were coming to hear of Amma. Others were in touch with the network of people I had met in the summer and, slowly but surely, a much wider circle of people pitched in to help host Amma's tour. The pre-tour idea had generated a lot of excitement as had been hoped. At the time the *First World Tour Souvenir* was published in May of 1987, after one year of organizing effort, 40 programs had been arranged representing the spiritual diversity of America:

THE HOLY MOTHER'S U.S. TOUR-1987

May 18	Mother's arrival at San Francisco Airport
May 19	The Yoga Society of San Francisco
May 20	Badarikashram, San Leandro, CA
May 21	Harwood Vipassana Meditation House, Oakland
May 22	Christ Episcopal Church, Sausalito, CA
May 23	First Unitarian Church, San Francisco

May 24   Cultural Integration Fellowship,
            San Francisco

May 25   Devi Bhava Darshan,
            The Rosner's Residence, Oakland

May 26   Unity Church, Santa Cruz, CA

May 27   The Women's Club of Carmel, CA

May 29   Quaker Friends Meeting House,
            Seattle, WA

May 30   Unity Church, Bellevue, WA

May 31   Devi Bhava Darshan, Terri Hoffman's
            Residence, Seattle

June 2   Melia Foundation, Berkeley, CA

June 3   Whispering Pines Lodge, Miranda, CA

June 4-6   Retreat at Morningstar Community,
            Mt. Shasta, CA

June 7   Devi Bhava Darshan,
            The Yurt at Morningstar, Mt. Shasta

June 9-10   The Great Hall at St. John's College,
            Santa Fe

June 12   The Center for Performing Arts, Taos,
            New Mexico

June 13   Harwood Auditorium, Taos

June 14   Temple Stones Blessing, the Longo-Whitelock
            Residence, Taos

June 15   The Pillai Residence, Albuquerque

June 16   The Lama Mountain Meditation Center,
            Lama Mountain, New Mexico

June 17 Devi Bhava Darshan, the Lipscomb-Ross
         Residence, Taos
June 19 The White Church on Quesnel, Taos
June 20 The Hanuman Temple, Taos
June 21 Solstice Celebration of the Divine Mother,
         hosted by Jameson Wells of Pot Creek, NM
June 22 The Stevens Residence, Carson, NM
June 23 Devi Bhava Darshan, the Schmidt Residence,
         Santa Fe
June 25 Gates of Heaven, Madison, Wisconsin
June 26 Quaker Friends Meeting House, Madison
June 27 Unitarian Church, Madison
June 28 Devi Bhava Darshan, the Lawrence Residence,
         Madison
June 29 Ramalayam Hindu Temple, Lemont, Illinois
July 1   Divine Life Church, Baltimore,
         Maryland
July 2   Unitarian Church, Washington DC
July 4   Plain Pond Farm, Providence,
         Rhode Island
July 5   Cambridge Zen Center, Cambridge,
         Massachusetts
July 6   The Sufi Order of Boston, Boston
July 7   The Theosophical Society, Boston
July 8   Harvard University, Cambridge
July 9   Old Cambridge Baptist Church,
         Cambridge

July 10 The Himalayan Institute,
          New York City
July 11 The Geeta Temple Ashram,
          Elmhurst, NY
July 12 St. John the Divine Cathedral,
          New York City
July 13-14 Retreat at the Devan Residence of
            Connecticut
July 15 Amma's departure for the Europe Tour

We wrapped up the end of the pre-tour on the East Coast and headed back just 10 days before Amma arrived. We had swept the path and it was time for the world to meet Amma at last. 🪔

CHAPTER SEVEN

On the World Stage

San Francisco
May 18, 1987

Finally the sun rose on the glorious day of Amma's arrival!
It was a beautiful, crisp day and all preparations for
Amma and the group had been made with utmost devotion and anticipation. Everything from Amma's darshan
chair to fresh vegetables, from new socks to fresh bedding
had been procured with everyone's help. We had rented a
white, 12-seater van for the drive across the Bay Bridge to
pick up Amma and the group. Many of the people who
had been helping with preparations joined us to welcome
Amma at the San Francisco International Airport.

There are no words to describe how my heart felt
that morning. All the care I had taken over the last year,
all the miles, all the trials and tribulations, all of Amma's
grace that had made this moment possible — it was all
reverberating within me. I scanned the faces of Amma's
children who were about to meet Her for the first time —
how hard they had worked, how soft and beautiful their
faces were in that moment of anticipation. The Rosners'

San Francisco Airport Darshan

son, Gabriel, had jumped into my arms to get a better look at Amma as she glided, as graceful as a swan, into the San Francisco Airport's arrival hall to meet us. Amma's face was as I had never seen it. She was always radiant and present, but this moment she was incandescent. Every particle of her being was aglow and pouring forth energy like a huge wave breaking on the shore.

AMMA IN THE HOUSE!

A garland was offered and someone had thought to bring a bag of chocolates — some Hershey's Kisses — which Amma began distributing, giving each person a hug and a Kiss. We all sat for some time near Amma while the bags were being collected and the vehicles brought around to the curb. Amma was just beaming, and all were hushed, basking in her glow, as if this moment would never end. Amma was so natural and conversing with everyone, asking their names and making everyone laugh with joy to hear Amma's voice for the first time, telling a story from the long journey.

Finally Amma and the group were in the white van, all the luggage had been accounted for, and the caravan headed east across the bay. I remember looking in the rearview mirror as I pulled away from the curbside; Amma settled back into her seat, quietly gazing out the window, taking in the view of America for the first time.

The very next morning Amma began giving darshan at the Rosner residence to a small group of eager devotees

who could not wait until the evening to attend Amma's first scheduled program. I especially remember the late Steve Fleischer and his wife, Marilyn Eto; Dennis and Bhakti Guest, who had somehow been guided to the house to meet Amma that first morning; and, of course, Tina, Nancy, George, Tim, Robin, James, Jack and Cherie, who had all helped so much the past year were also there.

Amma began with a long meditation, followed by a darshan session, punctuated by Amma singing simple namavali bhajans(devotional songs that repeat the names of the Lord), while embracing each person. After a few hours the program ended, and everyone disbanded to do some last-minute postering around town, and to get ready for the first night's program at the Yoga Society of San Francisco.

AMMA'S FIRST EVENING PROGRAM

San Francisco
May 19th 1987

It may sound strange, but I was tremendously nervous as I drove Amma and the group to San Francisco that first night. I remember looking down at my hands clutching the steering wheel as we crossed the Bay Bridge heading west; my knuckles were white from the intensity of my grip. "Deep breaths," I kept telling myself. "Just chant your mantra, keep chanting." Why was I so nervous? Considering all of the effort that had been made, my main doubts that night were: "Will anyone turn up? Will Amma be received properly? Will the Yoga Society be disappointed that they hosted Amma's program and the hall was not full?" Such thoughts were racing through my mind as I turned the corner to pull up in front of the hall.

What a sight met my eyes! People were lined up all the way down the block waiting to get in! A wave of relief swept over me, and I immediately relaxed, swinging out of the van to help Amma alight into a beautiful crowd of eagerness; someone garlanded Amma and we were led into the hall.

A small riser for a stage was just barely big enough to fit all of us, and that night, the only night ever in the US, Amma sang without a sound system. She tore the sky open with her singing and heaven fell down on us. "Gajanana He Gajanana," "Gopala Krishna," "Shristiyum Niye," "Karunalaye Devi," "Prabhu Misam" and "Durge Durge" — I can hear Amma singing them now, as if it were only yesterday. I kept peeking out at the audience to see the reaction. It is difficult to find words to describe that scene — the core group of people were all crowded in right up front, not even five feet away from Amma, swaying while she sang. Everyone's eyes were on Amma; they were transfixed and completely silent. Many of them had been singing devotional songs for more than a decade with other satsang groups, but some of their expressions belied the fact that they had never heard or felt anything like this in their life. Some in the audience, of course, had tears streaming down their cheeks, but the more prevalent expression was one of awe.

I had worked for a year with some of these folks, and had been looking forward to being there for their first darshan hug, but it looked like darshan had already started happening for some of them. Amma sang a long bhajan set, and no one moved from their spot. At the end, when the closing prayers had been chanted, there was a profound silence. We all sat and waited, not wanting to disturb the moment with movement. Afterwards Amma gave darshan late into the night. Many, many people had their first of what would become many chocolate Kisses from Amma that night in San Francisco, rocked gently in Amma's embrace, never to be the same again.

Driving back to Oakland, the monks brought up the topic of a sound system. It would not be possible, especially in this cold climate, for the bhajan sessions to be acoustic. Amma asked about the size of the other halls, and while describing their size, it became clear to me as well; we would need to travel with a sound system.

TESTING, TESTING, ONE-TWO, ONE-TWO...

The next morning found me driving into downtown Oakland to locate a music store, while the devotees gathered at the Rosner residence for morning meditation and darshan. Walking in wearing my white Punjabi set, I looked very out of place. It was a rock-n-roll music-supply store, and every square inch was covered with stuff. Hanging from the ceiling were electric guitars, ukuleles, saxophones, enormous speakers… You name it, it was in this store. Posters of rock stars and jazz musicians, many of them signed, plastered the walls. The glass display cases were crammed with every microphone you could ever want; cables, carrying crates, mic stands, black lights, dry-ice machines, mixers, amplifiers, big and small; it could all be purchased here. Feeling a little out of my element, and wishing I had not come alone, I approached the counter to get some assistance.

They had already spotted me. A salesman stood waiting. I smiled weakly and said, "Hi." My mouth felt dry, but I had to make this work. "I need a sound system."

"What kind of music?"

"East Indian devotional singing, harmonium, tablas, powerful vocals, sitting on the floor, travelling on tour."

The salesman seemed fine with that, nothing he hadn't heard before. "How much money do you want to spend?"

"Not too much."

"Live performance or a studio recording? Who's your sound engineer?"

"What's a sound engineer?"

That raised his eyebrow a bit. "How many musicians? Do you plan to do any recording?"

"Yes, most definitely."

The salesman scurried off into a back room. He soon returned and, clearing a space on a counter, he assembled a starter system for me in less than 20 minutes. He recommended a simple Peavey mixer with a built-in amp; great sound quality for a good value, it was reliable, easy-to-use, travelled well, and had 10 microphone inputs. Sold. Two speakers with stands, a set of vocal microphones and stands, cables, and made to order, heavy duty carrying cases. I picked orange for the color, those would be ready in a week. All still within budget. This guy was good. The last item was a microphone for Amma. For that I had set aside a little extra money. "Our lead singer, she has a powerful voice. And she sways when she sings," I heard myself saying.

He thought for a moment, then selected a microphone out of the display case and handed it to me. "This is the model that Aretha Franklin used for many years," he told me. "She would pick this microphone over more expensive ones because she liked the sound so much, it suited her voice."

He had me at "Aretha"; I bought it.

He asked again who would be the sound engineer. When I said it was me and that I had no experience, he nodded. Okay then, you will need to know how to operate it. So, I got a crash course on setting up the system, how to set the levels and balance the mixing, plus a few pointers on what to watch out for. On the first night we would skip the recording, he was pretty sure I had my plate full. When I got back to Amma's house, darshan had finished and the group was resting. I did an archana and prayed for a boon.

Driving to the hall with the newly purchased equipment, I met the devotees who had come in advance to help decorate the hall. They were all abuzz with their post-darshan happiness and couldn't have been more helpful. We carried in the sound system and gingerly took it out of the boxes. I tried to look like I knew what I was doing. While they tidied up the stage, decorated with flowers and arranged the altar, I began sweating the set-up. Carefully following the directions I had been given, methodically setting the microphones in place, not tangling the cables, making a mental note of which microphone was with which soundboard number, keeping Amma's mic-stand to the side so it would not be in front of her when she sat down, I felt satisfied. I had given my best effort; the outcome was in Amma's hands. To be detached and to remember, "I am not the doer," was all that remained to be done. I drove back just in time to pick up Amma and the group.

When we arrived at the hall, I jumped out of the van and asked one of the core group members to park it nearby. Leading Amma into the hall and up to the stage, I darted back to be ready to set her mic-stand in place. Amma bowed down, as she always does when taking her seat before a program. Then she slowly looked at all the people who had come for the program. It was a good-sized crowd and pin-drop silent. Amma looked over at me and made a minute gesture for the microphone, as if that was the typical thing I did next, to set the microphone for the

Goddess of the Universe. Chanting my mantra I placed the mic and looked to see how Amma was reacting. She raised the same eyebrow in the identical way the salesman had that same morning! I had to laugh a little under my breath, Amma never missed a beat! She was with us, watching us and watching over us at the same time, whether it was something big or something small. Her ability to confirm her constant presence through subtle communication was impeccable. However if we are not paying attention, it can be easily missed. Only a half-second had passed, and everything I needed to know had been communicated. Amma smiled so sweetly at me, reached out and gave her blessing by touching the top of my head. That was all I needed; my nervousness melted away. Taking my place at the mixing board, I slowly turned up the volume on each mic and breathed a sigh of relief. It all went off without a hitch. Amma's microphone was fantastic.

The Bay Area and Northern California were fortunate to enjoy nearly two weeks of Amma's programs that first year, as far north as Mount Shasta and as far south as Carmel. Amma was completely at ease wherever she was. Already a devoted entourage kept turning up at program after program, many of whom had attended the first video showing in San Francisco, almost a year ago to the day.

THE FIRST DEVI BHAVA

Amma's first-ever Devi Bhava darshan outside of Amritapuri took place in America at an unlikely venue. Early one morning, Amma came downstairs and was peering into each room of the Rosners' house. We didn't understand at first what Amma was looking for, but we would soon find out. No one had known whether or not Amma would hold a Devi Bhava outside of India, but that's what was on Amma's mind that morning. One side room of the house was about the size of the Kalari in Amritapuri, with two French doors opening out into a larger living room area. That was the room Amma picked.

The announcement was made during morning darshan and again at the evening program — Amma would sit for Devi Bhava the following evening starting at 8:30 pm. The next day, silk saris were hung all around as decoration while we searched for the right seat for Amma and a small side table to hold the prasad tray. A simple altar was arranged on the back wall with a picture of the Divine Mother and a brass oil lamp; a magnificent wildflower arrangement and fruit bowl provided the finishing touches. An earth-toned folk art mandala I had purchased in Kochi was hung as a backdrop.

Although 1987 was the pre-cell phone era and the news went out by word of mouth, many people began arriving in the late afternoon. Soon the house was filled to capacity with overflow spilling onto the grassy front yard. The monks had set up for *bhajans* in front of the 'temple doors,' which would soon swing open to reveal to the Western world for the first time the awe-inspiring vision of Amma in Devi Bhava.

When 8:30 approached, the devotional singing had been going strong for more than an hour, and the devotees' mood was full of anticipation. Three of us were inside the homemade temple with Amma getting ready. The pujari had brought a multi-tiered arati lamp, which was heaped with camphor. Amma's attendant was putting the finishing touches on everything while I polished the silver crown. Amma had selected a beautiful deep-green sari that night. Having placed the crown on the peetham for Amma's blessing, I stood alert, chanting my mantra intently, waiting for the signal to open the temple doors for the opening song of the Bhava Darshan, "Ambike Devi."

Although I had spent many a Devi Bhava with Amma in the Kalari in India, the feeling that night was distinctly different, as if a torrent of energy from deep within the earth was streaming into the room with a silent, palpable pulse. At last Amma was ready and took her seat, sitting with eyes closed on the *peetham* we had offered, holding flower petals in both hands, though subtly I could feel the sword and trident. Unfortunately the attendant had neglected to bring Amma's ankle bells, which was the first time that had ever happened! Amma was vibrating with tremendous speed and the air was becoming very heated, crackling with electricity. The arati lamp was lit when, unexpectedly, the room lurched slightly sideways and I recall thinking, "Oh no, is there an earthquake right now?" I looked at the other two people in the temple and they too had very serious looks on their faces, which was no comfort to me. What was going on?

When I looked at Amma, I realized that she was the source of the power surge; it was all emanating directly from her. I thought to myself, "Oh my! Amma is going to lift the house from its foundation!" At that same moment the blissful thought pervaded my mind that the most ancient Divine Mother of the Universe was manifesting in America at this very moment, piercing through the heavy material veil with tremendous, effortless force. An eternity passed before the room seemed to stabilize, and Amma gestured to open the temple doors. Camphor smoke was billowing in the air, and Amma was radiating indescribable heat and light and power such as I had never witnessed before. She began receiving the first devotees. It felt as if the whole earth had opened up and Amma was drawing that primordial energy into this place from the deepest, densest recesses of existence, bringing it to bear here in America. I remember thinking, "I don't think things here will ever be the same again."

In 1987, Amma sat for Devi Bhava in the most unexpected locations. In Mount Shasta, a yurt pitched in a meadow on a rising slope of the mountain was the setting, on a full-moon night no less! In Madison, Amma sat for the Bhava Darshan in a rustic dairy barn from the turn of the century on the Lawrence family property. The Schmidts' house, the Hoffmans', the Ross-Lipscombs', were all host to Devi as she blessed the devotees. There was no limitation for Amma to manifest the full, potent power of the Divine Mother. Her children were finding her at last, and she would wipe away their tears regardless of time or place.

MOUNT SHASTA

Mount Shasta is the Arunachala of California; a volcanic mountain, it is a place regarded by many as a holy mountain that personifies Lord Shiva. In 1986, through Larry Kelley, I had been put in touch with Susan Rajita Cappadocia, an exuberant 25-year-old, the same age as me. She felt connected to Amma right from the first video showing and made so much effort to bring Amma's first US tour to her hometown, Mount Shasta.

The Morningstar community where she lived was located on the rising slope of the mountain and afforded a breathtaking view. Amma's first daytime darshan programs were held there and it seemed that the whole town of Mount Shasta was making pilgrimage to Amma seated on their beloved mountain. Amma also enjoyed the beauty, pointing out various aspects of nature that were attracting her attention. After the program was concluded, Amma took a walk around the property and spied a yurt – a round, nomadic tent-like shelter pitched in a beautiful flowering meadow. After a few moments of checking the environs and peeking into the quaint canvas structure, Amma declared that she would sit for Devi Bhava in this spot the following evening on the full moon. The devotees' mood soared when they heard the translation of what Amma had just said.

The next day while Amma gave darshan, all our attention was focused on transforming the yurt into a temple. We began to get the site ready – shrubbery was carefully clipped back to make room for the devotees and tarps went down on the ground in front, an area just inside the front section of the yurt was arranged where the monks could lead the bhajans. We rolled back about half of the canvas that was lashed to the lattice-work walls to afford a view into the yurt-temple. Colorful silk saris were hung to decorate the interior and an elaborate altar was set up just behind Amma's peetham. About 200 people came for the opening ceremony and Rajita, writing years later, recalled, "When the curtains opened and I looked at Amma I saw a divine flame, her body vibrating as if a mighty rushing river was inside her. It was extremely powerful."

I felt tremendous joy seeing people connect with Amma in all her glory. Every mile, every missed meal, the exhaustion, even the loss of my visa — all that was worth it to see the reunion of Divine Mother and child. My instinct had been correct all along: there was a Divine Mother in this world, and her children were all finding her!

LEMONADE BY THE RIVER

Along the drive north from Santa Fe to Taos, there is a dangerous stretch of road that lies directly next to the Rio Grande. There are some places where there is not even room to pull off the road to change a tire — that's how close it is to the river. We were in the middle of that

10-mile stretch when Amma mentioned that she was very thirsty. I thought for a moment, but knew there was no shop or café for miles. Again Amma said she was so thirsty, what was to be done? Then I realized that we were almost at Meadow's house, the same friend who had told me about the "Divine Mother in India" so many years before. The bridge that marked the turn to her property came into view and, taking Amma's permission, I turned off the highway.

The bridge needs to be mentioned, as it was a very old, rickety-looking bridge made of wooden planks, with thick steel cables suspending it over the rushing river. I knew that although it looked flimsy, it was certified by the State Engineer each season to permit cars and trucks to pass over it. Seeing the condition of the bridge, the monks cried out, "Stop!" So I did, all the while explaining that it was safe. They forbid me from driving over it though, and so I parked the van and we all walked across the bridge with Amma.

Can you imagine the surprise of Meadow, Ajna and Riversong when they saw who was coming up their driveway? Meadow came running from the garden with the girls close behind. Amma hugged them all as the story of Meadow telling me about Amma tumbled out, with Amma smiling knowingly all the while. Seemingly by coincidence, they had just made a big jar of herbal sun tea. Glasses were brought out and we all sat to enjoy the sound of the river, the view of the colorful La Barranca cliffs just behind us, and the delicious, thirst-quenching sun tea. As I watched Meadow and her daughters basking in the bliss of Amma's presence, I knew that her repeated requests for something to drink had just been her way of bringing us to this spot, so that Meadow's prayers of one day meeting the Divine Mother in the flesh could be fulfilled. Over the years, I came to see that this was Amma's way — instead of making bold pronouncements that would reveal her omniscience, she would act as if she needed something small, or find some excuse to orchestrate events such that the innocent prayers of her children could be fulfilled, all the while masking her true power. There are many similar stories in the life of Sri Krishna. In fact, it is a testament to Amma's humility that she often goes out of her way to conceal her omniscience.

RUGGED MOMENTS

All things considered, everything went very smoothly throughout the first tour, except when it didn't. But the rugged moments were mile markers, huge tests for me and, in retrospect, they stand out as defining moments on my spiritual journey with Amma. These whoppers of mistakes brought me a heightened awareness on the spiritual path and forced me to correct myself accordingly.

One such moment arrived early on in the tour. We had been generously loaned a Westfalia Volkswagen van to make the drive to Miranda and Mount Shasta by Dennis and Bhakti Guest of Orinda. It was a long drive from the

Bay Area to Miranda, and having the extra vehicle meant that there was a bit more space for Amma and everyone to spread out. The drive was incredibly gorgeous, but sinuous, as we wended our way from Miranda to Mount Shasta. My first mistake came in not being careful when picking the route. Yes, on the map the route was the shortest distance between the two points, but in actuality the road was a torture for everyone. More than three hours of torture. Everyone except me, the driver, became car-sick, and as much as we all wanted the drive to finish as quickly as possible, driving fast was not an option on a two-lane twisting back road.

As the miles crawled by, my mental agony increased in direct proportion to the groans coming from the back of the van; if only I had checked more carefully for a more mellow alternate route. I vowed to myself that from now on I would consult the local devotees when it came to choosing a route. For the moment, there was nothing I could do except focus on the road ahead of me and try to smooth out my driving on the unfamiliar terrain. But the worst was yet to come.

When we finally reached the Mount Shasta area, I took the wrong exit, not having written down the precise directions that had been given by the devotee whose home Amma would be staying in. Gulp. That I was lacking awareness when making the arrangements for this leg of the journey was the understatement of the year! Remember there was no such convenience as a cell phone to put out an S.O.S. call. I backtracked on I-5 and somehow recalled the exit was "Edgewood-Weed," not Mount Shasta. After I exited, an oncoming car was flashing its headlights at me; it was a devotee from the area and she had spotted us. At least someone was paying attention! I pulled off the road into a grassy rest area and waited for the devotee to turn around and catch up with us.

At that moment Amma started reprimanding me: Did I know where we were going or not? Why had I not been more careful when making arrangements? There was nothing I could say. Amma was right. I had not been alert, not taken care with the details. When Amma scolds one of her disciples the words have real power — the power of the universe. It can shake you to the core. It makes a deep impression. This is intentional because she wants to make an impression — one that will transform that person and make him or her more alert in the future. *Sraddha* — alertness — is essential for a spiritual seeker. Without it, one can never make any progress. For how can one transform their negative actions, words and thoughts if they are not alert enough to notice their presence in the first place? I understood all this, but part of me did not accept it. Part of me felt, "Come on! It's not my fault. These things happen." Perhaps it was because I did not fully accept Amma's teaching that the next thing happened.

By that point, the devotees had driven into the pull-out lane and were gesturing to me to follow them. I put the van in reverse and was backing up when suddenly

"BANG" — we hit something. Everyone exclaimed loudly, and I turned off the ignition, set the emergency brake and jumped out of the van to have a look. Hidden in the tall grass was a metal post about a meter high. There was a big dent in the back bumper. What was that post doing there? I didn't know, but the image of the unperturbed steel hit home. Steady mind, steady progress. At least I could learn from a steel post what I couldn't learn from my teacher. When I climbed back in the van, Amma was smiling. She told me not to worry; I had cured everyone's car-sickness!

Getting lost along the way can happen — but paying attention to details would have prevented that in the first place. Accepting whatever comes, praise or blame, with a steady mind, that was the other lesson for me. I had fervently prayed to reach the goal of spiritual life; in order for that to happen I would need to lose my sense of ego and pride. It's a rugged sport, no doubt, but that's what it takes to reach the goal. We won't learn by being given lollypops when we mess up.

When Amma saw a disciple lacking awareness, and retaining their complacency after she pointed it out, then she was only doing her job to be strict on these points. Amma takes her role as teacher seriously; the more we long to reach the goal, the stricter she will be to root out our negativities. But we must also play our role of disciple equally well – with earnestness and sincerity to change our character. If Amma brings something to our attention that needs corrected, we must be ready to change. Otherwise we are wasting everyone's time.

It seemed to me that being with Amma shed light on the best and the worst in a person. Amma's presence can be compared to pouring fresh water into a dirty bottle. Initially, the dirt comes out. It is only afterwards that the clear water will remain clear. That process can take a long time to be complete, depending on how much dirt is in the bottle, even multiple lifetimes. One should have the grace and insight to understand what is happening and to confront the dirt and throw it out for good.

Amma will fulfill the purpose of why we came to her – she will take us to the goal – by being attentive to the wandering mind of her student. But as it is with bad habits and slow learners, it would take another big bump in the road to really hit it home for me.

That happened in New Mexico. Amma had arrived in Taos, and the evening program at the Harwood Auditorium was well-attended. The place we were to stay in that night was out on the Taos Mesa, and the person who had offered their house for Amma and the group was out of town at the time. I had delegated the house preparation to another local couple, while I was busy with the details of the evening program. However, when we arrived late in the night after a long darshan, it was clear that the house was not ready. That night was destined to be the worst night of the whole tour for me.

When we pulled up, there was no one to greet us — the house was locked and dark. I wondered if I had gone to the wrong place. But no, here came the couple I had delegated the preparation to, driving up the driveway. My relief was short-lived, however. After they led us into the house, I glanced in at the kitchen. There were dirty dishes in the sink. Showing Amma to the bedroom, I cringed to see that the beds were not even made up. The house was not prepared even to receive an ordinary houseguest, let alone the Divine Mother. Not that those things matter to Amma in the slightest, but I was mortified that I had totally neglected my duty to do the final check and verify that the accommodation was all set up. Not a small detail in the least, but there was nothing to be done about it at 3:00 in the morning. Amma endured this experience without comment, sat down to read her mail and have dinner.

Amma could gauge my inner awareness and observed that I did not need a scolding; I had extracted the lesson from the situation already. Knowing that my lack of awareness had practically left Amma out on the street was unbearable to me. But the young woman who has since left Amma was merciless. I have to admit that although I was remorseful, hearing her stinging words, I still retained a hint of the "I'm-doing-the-best-I-can" attitude.

The good news is: that never happened again. The bad news is: the next day culminated in a series of choices that made the lesson all the more powerful. Leaving behind the dirty, ill-equipped house, we drove to a beautiful location in the Lama Mountains, about 15 miles north of Taos. At least the road was not winding, but it was long. Many devotees drove all the way from Santa Fe and Colorado just to attend this program on Lama Mountain, as it was known for its tranquility and was where a Sufi master had spent time teaching and had his tomb.

Still rattled from the disaster of the night before, I searched out a friend, Rita Sutcliffe, to see if her house was available after the morning program for Amma to rest in. She heartily agreed and raced back home, missing the morning's glorious darshan program to make sure everything was picture perfect for Amma and the group. Satisfied that last night's fiasco would not repeat itself, I did not see that my taking matters into my own hands without checking with Amma was creating another blind spot that would cause a bigger problem later. In that moment I should have let Amma know that an alternate house was being arranged in town, close to the evening venue. But I didn't because I thought I was in control of the situation, no problem.

Around noon there were still a lot of people waiting for darshan when a man approached me. He introduced himself as Richard Schiffman and said that Amma had agreed to come to his house further up the mountain before the evening program. Even though I knew that Rita's house was in the process of being prepared for Amma's arrival, I asked him about his place, mainly to be polite.

He told me it was a small rustic cabin, with no running water, about 20 minutes further up the mountain on a dirt road. Yikes! There was no way I was going to bring Amma and the group there after what had happened the night before. I explained to him that some other arrangements were already being made and it would not be possible to bring Amma to his cabin. Mistake number two: I should have checked with Amma to find out what she had promised Richard.

The morning program ended and we began wending our way down the Lama Mountain road and turned onto the highway heading south. We had travelled less than a mile when Amma asked where we were going. When I explained about the new arrangement, Amma asked me why we were not going to Richard's house, hadn't he informed me of Amma's wish to rest there? I said yes, but as he didn't have running water, and it was 20 minutes up a dirt road in the wrong direction, I had decided that the house in town was a better choice. The monk who is now Swami Poornamritananda had been translating all this time, but now he paused. "You did what, Kusuma?" he asked me softly. I repeated myself, thinking he had not heard clearly. He remained silent, not wanting to translate such indiscrimination.

Amma didn't need a translation to know what had happened and the silence of the night before would have been a welcome balm to the scolding I got. In my rush to correct the mistake I made the night before, I made a bigger blunder — I had forgotten that what was really important to Amma was spiritual growth — mine and everyone else's. Of course I knew full well that the purpose of life with a Guru is to transcend one's ego and sense of self as a limited individual and that one does not do that by making decisions for the Guru.

Worse still, Amma had given her word to Richard that she would visit his house and now, through my thoughtless action, I had prevented Amma from fulfilling his wish. Amma had given her word, and I had blocked it. She could not be shy to show me what I had done. If I persisted in this habit, I would continue to make more problems for myself and others; Amma was going to nip that tendency in the bud immediately.

In a way it was good that I was driving, because if I had been seated near Amma looking at her I think I might have died. It hit me, the lesson, like a wrecking ball. Amma declared that she would not continue the tour any longer with me in charge, someone else should take over. No one breathed. When we pulled up at the devotee's home, they came running out to welcome Amma with innocent smiles and a beautiful garland. One of the monks got out of the van and explained that Amma would come in a moment, that we were finishing a discussion.

I dragged myself out of the driver's seat and stood before Amma, and begged her forgiveness. I appreciated Amma for being so sincere in her role as Guru and hoped that I would become a more receptive student. If we are drowning in the sea and the lifeguard comes to save us, what is the meaning in climbing up on top of him and yelling out, "Someone save me!" Surrender yourself to him, and let him pull you to the shore. Amma was saving me and the least I could do was let myself be saved! I solemnly promised to check with Amma about all tour-related details, especially if anyone came and said that Amma had told them she would pay a house call.

The anger of a true master like Amma has been compared to a burnt rope — it looks solid, but when touched, it crumbles to ashes. Many times I have seen Amma appear to be angry in one moment and beaming and laughing the next. Or scolding a disciple severely, only to look at them with love and concern as soon as they turn to walk away. Even in those days, after just a few years with Amma, I *knew* that Amma is never really angry, and makes use of a show of anger for the good of her disciples. When she wants her disciples to be aware they have made a mistake, they will feel it. But Amma doesn't hold onto things — once the lesson has been learned, or at least received without internal resistance, it is over, her apparent anger vanishes, just as a candle flame is blown out by the wind. It can look ferocious, Amma's anger, but doesn't a mother have to scold her children, to make them alert and aware, so that they don't make bigger mistakes in the future? In fact, Amma's reprimands, tempered by her motherly love, have produced a group of senior disciples who are amazingly down-to-earth, approachable, and realistic about their own shortcomings. They are able to laugh at themselves, even after all these years.

HIGH POINTS IN THE SOUTHERN ROCKIES

Somehow I found the strength to keep moving forward with the tour. What choice was there? I couldn't dwell on my errors. Indeed, the point was not to fall prey to them again. I prayed to become the one who would thank Amma for pointing out where I could improve, not the one who resisted Amma's teaching. But it wasn't easy. The ego is a tough patron to dislodge once he makes himself comfortable!

The young woman who later left the ashram was known for her intense love of Amma, her dedication and self-sacrifice. But at the same time, those who knew her well were painfully aware of her emotional immaturity and unjustified criticism of others with a razor-sharp tongue, even to their face. She had a stubborn character, unable to hear criticism regarding her own shortcomings and seemed to resist taking the necessary steps to improve. She was an odd combination of intransigence and devotion. But why resist changing? I didn't want to be like that, it would only impede my progress on the path. Besides, it was painful and embarrassing to make the same mistake over and over.

HANUMAN HOUSE CALL

One unscheduled stop was all it took to get me back on

track. Since we were still in the Taos area, I had been sharing stories of special places, the Hanuman Temple being my favorite. Amma became very animated and insisted that we make a detour to go and pay our respects to Hanuman, the Lord's greatest devotee. So, we drove over to the temple and parked without any fanfare. Amma entered the shrine room and sat quietly in the middle of the room. The white marble *murti* (the statue of the deity) was from Jaipur and depicted Hanuman flying through the air holding a mace on his shoulder and Lord Rama's ring in his hand. Hanuman's face wore an expression of devotion and peace. Amma sat gazing at his visage with evident delight. The larger-than-life, two-ton statue was a masterpiece, magnificently displayed on the broad altar strewn with flowers, brass *puja* articles, burning candles and bowls of *prasad*. Somehow word had spread and devotees came out of the woodwork. The monks brought in the harmonium and a *mridangam* (a two-faced drum), and Amma began to sing—"Sri Rama Jaya Rama," followed by "Sita Ram Bol" and finished the set with "Mano Buddhyahamkara." Amma gave darshan to the 30 or so lucky souls to be in attendance, and then departed from the temple as quietly as she had come.

SANTA FE CHARM

The Schmidt family was remarkable from the moment I met them to do the first video showing of "A Day With Mother" in their home back in 1986. Steve was a prominent lawyer and Cathy (now Amrita Priya) was a music teacher; they are some of the most down-to-earth, hard-working, cheerful people I have ever met. Their young children, Sanjay and Devi, were darling and inquisitive. Their adobe home, nestled in the foothills of the Santa Fe Wilderness Area, had a meditation room that sat about 20 people comfortably. I noticed right away that the energy was so peaceful; they had done a lot of meditation. This was in fact the same family who had spontaneously called me in Boston just before the pre-tour to make a generous donation.

I was not at all surprised one morning when Amma started peeking into the rooms of their house, a telltale sign that something cosmic was brewing. She called all of us into the large, open living room area to ask if it would be alright to hang a curtain there to create the space for a small temple. The look on Steve and Cathy's faces was pure delight.

We started immediately – clearing the extensive collection of Kachina dolls from the mantle of the fireplace, moving out furniture and selecting the perfect chair for Amma to be seated on. Somehow word spread, and the next night the crowd of people thronging their property had to be managed both for car parking and the seating of all the people! I remember looking at Steve's reaction a few different times throughout the night; he was looking more and more wonderstruck and blissful. Cathy was the kindest hostess who didn't stop serving the devotees until each need had been met, and she continues on in this way to the present day.

It is their property that was destined to become the home for "Amma Center New Mexico" within a few years, and continues to be one of Amma's residential overseas ashrams known for its many long-term service projects such as feeding the homeless from 'Amma's Kitchen,' and working in the prisons to teach meditation. Similar to the San Ramon Ashram, the Santa Fe Amma Center also has a strong connection to Mother Nature expressed through their caretaking of organic vegetable gardens and a solar greenhouse, and well as leading training workshops for the community to learn about vegetable gardening in a high-mountain desert ecosystem.

SUMMER SOLSTICE, 1987

A special program for June 21st had been arranged at a meadow along the Pot Creek River just east of Taos. The property was owned by a local artist, Jameson Wells, who had carved a four-sided statue out of black granite that was her representation of the Goddess Kali. It was announced as a "Solstice Celebration of the Divine Mother," and we had painted seven square plaques white with a red triangle and a center dot on them to represent the seven sacred *chakras* (energy centers in the body). They were laid out in a line with the sculpture at the head. The family had pitched a yellow-and-white canopy to provide shade, but so many people had turned up that there was no respite from the burning mid-day sun. Amma wasn't satisfied with the seven chakra layout, and asked everyone to squeeze in under the canopy as tightly as possible, and to visualize the Divine Mother within themselves instead. I didn't know it at the time, but this was the commencement of the Devi Puja (Worship of the Divine Mother), later to become the Atma Puja(Worship of the Self), which would precede all of Amma's overseas Devi Bhava Darshan programs to this day. Amma conferred with the monks for a few moments while the devotees were regrouping under the canopy as best they could. Amma explained that we would chant 108 Names of Devi in the traditional call-and-response style. She instructed us to do the worship mentally. She said that *manasa puja* (mental worship) could be even more powerful than external worship if done with the attitude of surrender and enthusiasm. The monk would chant the first name, and we would chant back, *Om para shaktyai namaha* — I bow down to the Supreme Energy in the form of the Divine Mother — while making a gesture by placing our right hand at the heart and plucking a flower to offer to Devi. This was done to represent making an offering of our heart to the Divine. Amma also mentioned that if someone did not want to imagine the Divine Mother, they just could imagine an ideal, such as world peace or Mother Nature, instead. "Believe in your own Self and move forward on the path," Amma would always say.

Everyone had been paying keen attention to the translation, and we practiced together, with Amma leading us in the Om para-saktyai namaha response several times, while coordinating the offering of the lotus of the heart. It was so poetic, spontaneous and clear; by the time the ceremony had finished the mood was transcendent. No one had ever experienced anything quite like it, including me! Then Amma sang a few bhajans — "Kali Durge Namo Nama," "Para Shakti, Param Jyoti" — and gave darshan to everyone. The whole afternoon passed by blissfully, and soon it was time to bid farewell to the lovely gathering of devotees, many of whom would follow Amma to Madison a few days later.

MAGNIFICENT MADISON

The memorable pre-tour moments in Madison had set the stage for Amma's remarkable first year's program there. In many ways it felt like going to see old friends when we arrived to stay at the Lawrence family's 60-acre farm in the rolling woodlands just outside the city of Madison. And they were old friends; Barbara Lawrence was Swami Paramatmananda's first hatha yoga teacher and had given him his first copy of the Bhagavad Gita more than 20 years ago. Her daughter, Rasya, who lives with Amma in India today, recalls her mom saying about her young yoga student, "He would make a good monk."

Their fields were planted with alfalfa and Amma remarked about the majestic beauty of the maple trees. The Lawrence's turn-of-the-century dairy barn would be transformed into a temple for Amma's Devi Bhava Darshan a few days later. Swinging open the barn doors after an intense cleaning session with dozens of new devotees pitching in, the unbelievable beauty of the Devi Bhava scene rivaled that of the soaring maple trees.

Mary La Mar and Michael Price, also of Madison, hosted a wonderful daytime darshan for Amma in their spacious home. They were the other family who had contacted me in Boston to donate during my pre-tour moment of crisis. Naturally warm and friendly, looking after all the needs of those who came to meet Amma, Michael and Mary fit the bill of Midwestern hospitality to a T.

The outpouring of love during this 'Heartland' tour stop brought tears to my eyes on many occasions. The Sufi community hosted one of Amma's evening programs at the Gates of Heaven and I can still recall the group 'Jaya' singing their hearts out. One of the children of a family that attended the first video showing I did in 1986 was eight years old at the time. Vinay has been one of the residents at Amma's ashram in India for many years and spends all his time and creative energy on "Embracing the World," the umbrella organization for Amma's vast network of charitable activities around the world.

CLOSING MOMENTS OF THE FIRST US TOUR

The stories from the first US tour can go on and on, but I will save that for another volume. The joy of Amma with her children was its constant underlying melody; the profound beauty that had been brought into so many peoples' lives was transformative. Now it was almost time for Amma to fly to Paris and complete the last leg of her first world tour. The end point for this portion was in Connecticut at the home of the Devan family. For me it was excruciating. I had managed the tour on a shoestring budget. Every need had been met, but now every penny was spent. I had no visa to return to India. Amma was encouraging me to continue on to Europe, but I knew it was not possible.

In the morning I explained to one of the monks that I would take a job somewhere to pay back the debt, as I had promised, and that I had had to give up my entry visa in order to come back to plan the US tour. I had not had a chance to tell Amma all these details with all the hurry-burry of the tour; plus, it was a bit of a mood spoiler for me anyhow. The way it had all come together, that was a conscious choice I had made, it was what I had been willing to sacrifice to make sure the tour happened. The fulfillment for me was to see Amma with her children. Why fret about it now? I was sure that within six months I would be able to make it back to Amma in India, and in the meantime there was plenty of organizing to do for next year's tour, which Amma had already confirmed with the devotees.

When Amma heard from the monks what had happened, she had a different idea and called me to sit quietly with her. Amma asked me to share my story with the handful of devotees who had lingered on these last two days to say goodbye to Amma. She said that it was important for me to tell my story and then let whatever happened, happen. So I did just that. A small circle of us sat and I told my story. How important it had been for me to bring Amma to meet her children. How my own life had been immeasurably changed by Amma since meeting her, and I wanted that for others. But also in bringing Amma to America I had grown in my commitment to my own spiritual life, seeing how much need there was for a Realized Master to come and lead us to Truth. I talked for 10 or 15 minutes at most, keeping my gaze down all the while. I couldn't bear to see how people might react. When I finished I bowed down to the circle of people and got up to excuse myself. I noticed several of them wiping tears from their cheeks. They straight away invited me back to the Bay Area to stay in their homes and pledged to help in whatever way they could. They wanted to be part of next year's planning and were ready to start at a moment's notice.

One of the devotees went off to make arrangements for me to travel back with their family without further ado.

When I went back to Amma's room to tell her what happened, she had been waiting for me to serve her meal. I was looking forlorn when Amma mischievously remarked, "Why so sad?"

I replied, "Because Amma is going."

Amma immediately replied, "Where?"

Amma always says where there is love, there is no distance. And I had experienced that truth in profound ways, but in that moment I felt in despair to see Amma flying off, not knowing when I would "see" her again.

CHAPTER EIGHT

Going With The Flow...

I was able to get back to India much sooner than expected. After Amma departed for Europe, I flew back to the Bay Area with some of the devotees. My plan was to earn the money needed to pay back the debt as quickly as possible and spend as much time as I could with the devotees to keep the momentum going that Amma had created on tour. We started the first M.A. Center satsang group, which would meet each week at Hari Sudha's (Tina's) house in Berkeley. The evening would start with a video clip from Amma's recent tour; next we would offer the 108 Names of the Divine Mother, selected from the Lalita Sahasranama, which we had chanted with Amma all through the summer. We would sing bhajans for the better part of an hour, and end with a 15-minute silent meditation. Afterwards we would enjoy a potluck and people would stay late to hear Amma stories and ask questions. Devotees drove from all over the Bay Area to attend the weekly satsang in Berkeley, and sometimes they would invite me to do the same in their homes in Marin, Orinda, the South Bay or in San Francisco. It was a time of spontaneity and an outpouring of enthusiasm; everyone wanted to help make sure Amma would return the following year. Before long, weekly satsang groups were established in all these places.

The job I had planned to get never happened as my debt was cleared by devotees who insisted on remaining anonymous. A plane ticket was also provided for me to return to India; as it was by Amma's grace that it all happened this way, I gratefully accepted. By mid-August I was back with Amma. My sadhana and cozy hut next to the Kalari were like old friends welcoming me home.

CELEBRATING AMMA'S 34TH BIRTHDAY

In India it is customary to celebrate one's birthday on the day of one's birth star in month in which one was born. Thus it was that on October 10th we celebrated Amma's 34th birthday. Amma's birth star, Kartika, was overhead and the whole prayer hall of the nearly completed Kali Temple was filled with thousands of devotees just as Amma had foretold. How had Amma known to start the construction of the Kali Temple at the exact right moment in early 1986? That detail has always puzzled me. During this celebration, the "Mata Amritanandamayi Astottara Sata Namavali," or the 108 Names of Amma, composed by the elderly resident, lifelong *brahmacharin*(celibate monk), and poet laureate Ottur Namboodiri, were chanted for the first time while the *pada puja* (the washing of the feet of the Guru) went on. A new era dawned that day for Amma and her children. A shift from the solitude of the past years could be felt, though Amma remained the same pure soul as ever, caring for the devotees and bringing peace and joy to all who came in her midst, she was now more than ever, Mother of the World.

TOURING WITH AMMA

Amma and the ever-increasing number of ashram residents began touring more extensively in India, touching all parts of Kerala, and on into Tamil Nadu. We had outgrown the mini-bus and a larger bus was donated. In November we travelled to Mumbai for Amma's first-ever visit. As I sat behind Amma — hour after hour, day after day, quietly observing her divine presence bring beauty to all of the faces of those who passed through her loving arms — I marveled at her stamina. Even at the program's end, Amma would make a beeline to whatever room had been arranged for her and begin to read all her mail, meet with the local organizers or take time for any ashramites who needed guidance. Amma's tireless cheer was boundless. Each of us helped in some small way, but not one of us could keep up with Amma. I would sit for hours waving the hand fan if it was hot, trying to convince Amma to drink some water, and keeping a fresh face towel handy. At the end of darshan, which had gone on throughout the day, while I was ready to rest, Amma would jump in a waiting car to go do 10 house calls until dawn broke. All the while creating a mood of laughter and delight, but watching the minds of the disciples to correct any missteps. Amma was an ocean of compassion, on stage and off.

All of the programs around India were well-planned, and many people were able to meet Amma for the first time. I learned some important details by watching Amma guide the local organizers: to always include people in whatever way they wanted to help, never turning anyone away, always welcoming new people with a smile and following up to make sure all had been fed and had a place to rest. After we returned to Kerala, many more devotees began making the pilgrimage to the ashram and all the rooms in the Kali Temple prayer hall were filled up as fast as they were made ready.

INTROSPECTION

I had returned to India on a three-month tourist visa and in November I would have to apply for a three-month extension, which was permitted in those days. I could only hope the Foreigner's Registration Office had forgiven me and that I was in their good graces again, as I couldn't bear the thought of having to leave after 90 days. Because of this, each day felt like a gift, and I took nothing for granted. Each night I would introspect and try to clearly understand my shortcomings. Had I been patient, had I been kind? Had I had enough awareness and mantra japa going continuously, as those had been problem areas for me during the tour. Had my archana been properly offered? If not, I would chant once more before sleeping. Had I been able to help someone, even if it was in a small way? Had I remembered Mother Earth and done something for her betterment? Had my heart drawn closer to Amma today? During the tour Amma had instructed me in this way, and I knew it was as important as drinking water.

The young woman who is no longer at the ashram seemed to be jealous of me, and I tried not to let that affect me. My service was an offering of love, and I wanted to be aware not to let my own pride feed into that dynamic. I didn't want to get on her bad side, as I had observed that she could make life difficult by blocking access to Amma for people who were not in her good graces. It was inevitable that anger, jealousy, pride and judgment would come up around Amma; those were the very negativities we were trying to purify ourselves of! Practicing introspection helped me to see my part in situations and set things right. When I talked to Amma about the brewing situation, she pointed out that working to improve myself was my duty, while worrying about what someone else was doing was not. Amma made the point very clearly.

Amma would often use the metaphor of a rock tumbler to describe the situations we found ourselves in as we tried to reach the goal while living in a spiritual community. The rough edges of one stone would rub down the sharp points of the other stones; as they went around and around in the tumbler, each stone would become polished to perfection.

A NEW SEVA

Amma had switched my seva from cooking in the kitchen

to editing the new English books that were due to come out. *Mata Amritanandamayi: A Biography* was the first one, followed by *For My Children*, a collection of Amma's sayings arranged by themes. I also helped edit *On the Road to Freedom*, written by Swami Paramatmananda. In addition, each month I would send new material for the *Amritanandam* newsletter and the new issue's cover with Amma's photo to the M.A.Center devotees, who would photocopy it and post it to the 100 or so subscribers. In order to write the articles, I asked Amma if I could sit with a tape recorder and could ask her questions, which she answered on the spot. Each issue was dense with wisdom, sweetness and humor. Amma was pure satsang when it came to expressing spiritual wisdom and her talks would effortlessly take form in the moment. There was no intermediary, just pure Amma, which continues to this day.

THE "AMRITANJALI" SERIES

Recordings of all the bhajans were done in an improvised studio which was created in the small house that a Dutch devotee had built early on; the present location of the Vishuddhi Ayurvedic Clinic, just next to the northern entrance to the ashram. Everything was soundproofed as much as possible; reel-to-reel tape recorders were set up in the side room. Even in those days, when Amma would sit for a recording session, it would go on for one or two weeks! She and the whole ashram would become completely absorbed in the process. An incredibly charged atmosphere was created after hours and hours of sitting and singing with Amma. Over a period of about three years, 10 volumes of bhajans had been recorded for the original *Amritanjali* series. It's hard to imagine, but now, in 2012, Amma has recorded well over 1,000 songs in 35 languages!

The sales of the cassettes enabled Amma to start service projects for the poor and needy, the heart of her life's focus. The beautiful recordings of Amma and the ashramites singing not only gave the devotees a chance to listen to Amma's powerful bhajans when they were away from the ashram, her teachings were all in the songs as well, constantly reminding us of the way to reach the goal. No matter who wrote the songs, all the proceeds from the sales went towards launching some of the original service projects, which continue to this day, such as a free medical dispensary and primary care clinic, scholarships for needy students and the rescue of 500 children stranded in a financially failing orphanage in a nearby town.

SINGING MY SONG

New songs were coming out all the time. As the ashram atmosphere was so conducive for composing devotional hymns, there was no end to the stream of music. I continued to write a few songs here and there, but was too shy to sing them. One evening Amma got up from singing bhajans at the Kalari to roam around. As she walked away she instructed each one to sing. When my turn came, I leaned towards the harmonium player and whispered, "Iswari Jagad Iswari." It was my debut performance since singing, "Rain, Rain, Go Away" so many years ago. As the opening notes were played, I steadied myself and gave it all the devotion and concentration I could.

I had sung that song so many times while travelling to arrange the world tours that the five verses were etched in my memory. Everyone sang the chorus, but the verses were mine to sing alone. What a feeling of bliss to sing Amma's song! Years later I found out that Amma had been sitting nearby on the front steps of her family home and had asked, "Who's that singing?" and the person sitting with her replied, "Kusuma." To which Amma said, "But you told me she couldn't sing!"

iswari jagad iswari paripalaki karunakari
sasvata mukti dayaki mama
khedamokke ozhikkanne

O Goddess, O Goddess of the Universe,
O Preserver, O Giver of Grace and eternal
Liberation, please rid me of all my sorrows...

PLANNING THE 1988 US TOUR

By February it was time to go back to America and get ready for Amma's second summer tour. Amma had accepted invitations to visit two new places: Boulder, Colorado, where Swami Paramatmananda's sister lived, and Temple, New Hampshire, where a devotee family, Jani and Ganganath McGill, had a healing center, in addition to the other 12 cities and towns on the schedule already. Amma had agreed to my suggestion to hold meditation retreats in a few locations as well, so there was quite a bit of planning to do. This year no pre-tour was needed, but now I would go in advance to visit each tour stop and meet with the devotees to plan for Amma's 1988 US Tour. We would go around together locating the halls and possible retreat sites. What a difference a year with Amma had made for everyone! There was such a unity of purpose and excitement knowing what it meant for Amma to come a second time.

LET COME WHAT MAY

In each city and town I visited, a showing of "A Day With Mother" would be scheduled and I would cook a benefit dinner to help raise money for the tour. Sometimes local musicians and performing artists would organize a benefit performance, or artists and professionals would hold a silent auction and offer their art or services. People who had the financial means to contribute would, of their own accord. There was no pitch made for contributions. If people inquired about donating, beyond a simple explanation of Amma's ashram in India and the charitable activities that were already going on, I didn't feel to elaborate. Even today, in a 10,000 square-foot hall, there might be two small donation boxes set out. An often-asked question was, "Where can a donation be made?" because it was never obvious.

I had come up with the idea of printing envelopes for the Devi/Atma Puja ceremony, which was held on the last night of Amma's program in each city. It was in response to so many people asking that there be some way to quietly offer a donation at the end of Amma's visit. There was no charge for any of Amma's programs, and the retreat fees were kept at cost, providing three days of accommodation and food for all who attended. Even nowadays in the era of over-priced spiritual seminars that abound, Amma's retreats continue to be affordable. I managed everything on a shoestring budget, and somehow the expenses were always matched by enough contributions to cover what was needed for hall rentals, food, modest publicity and travel expenses. Amma's words, "Ask for nothing and everything will come," always came true.

PADA PUJA AND ARATI

I added two traditional practices to each day's program, washing Amma's feet when she entered the hall and performing the *arati* (waving of burning camphor before the deity) at the end of the evening program. Amma was not really keen for this, but when I insisted that the devotees would be so happy to get a chance to express their love and devotion, Amma finally agreed. A simple brass tray was used for the arati and the items used for the washing of Amma's feet were also made of simple brass or steel. I would go over the different steps involved in both of these devotional rituals when visiting the various cities. I felt

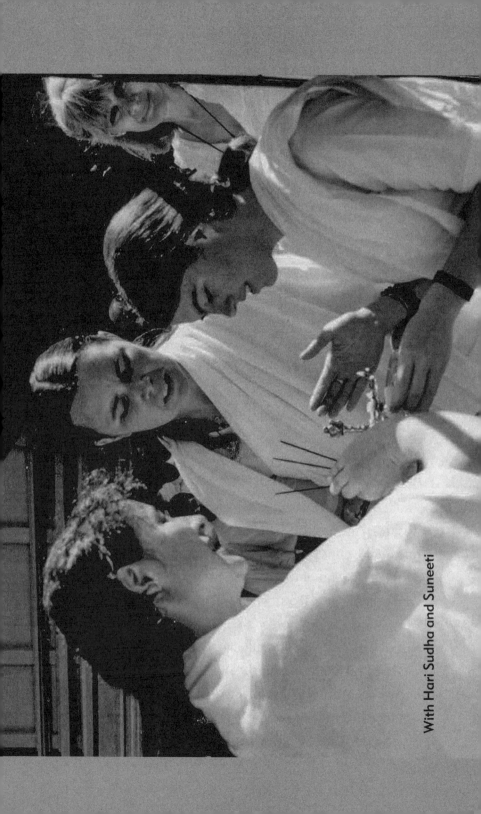

With Hari Sudha and Suneeti

that each one of Amma's children should get a chance if they wanted to, as it would inevitably draw them closer to Amma; these would be lifetime memories. We kept it very simple, but the deeper meaning behind it was explained and everyone got a turn.

Those ceremonies still go on throughout Amma's world tours and have brought so much joy for the devotees. On the path of love, it is through loving worship that the constant remembrance of the beloved eventually awakens our Oneness. It is not that the Guru needs this worship from us. Amma often says that the sun does not need the light of a candle to shine; in the same way God and Guru do not need us to worship them, it is for our benefit that we worship, as this process purifies our mind and brings us ever closer to our own true nature. Actions that bring out love and reverence for the Guru and the Truth in which the Guru is established are purifying and create a deep bond. This is the quintessence of the path of love.

1988 VOLUNTEER TOUR STAFF

Although we had no formal staff to accompany the tour, a group of ardent devotees was coalescing and would make themselves available in as many cities as they could to help with the advance preparations and throughout the summer tour. Tina and Nancy, who had by then become Hari Sudha and Suneeti, made it all the way to the East Coast, helping set up the halls and Devi Bhava Temple decorations, among other things. Ron Gottsegen of

Carmel was not going to miss a single city this tour, and he began helping at the sound board doing the recordings and the mixing. Ron was ready to do whatever was needed, whether that meant running out to the store to pick up some vegetables to cook for lunch, driving Amma and the monks back and forth from the hall, or helping to coordinate logistics at the airports. He was so cheerful and easy to work with, his quiet humor and demeanor had Amma in stitches many times along the way. We had two volunteer drivers, Scott Stevens and Ramana Erickson who drove across the country in a red Chevy pick-up truck with the 'Om-Zia' symbol painted on its doors to transport all the equipment and supplies. The truck had been generously donated by Sheila Guzman to use for the duration of the 1988 US tour.

The Om-Zia symbol bears mentioning because it was an icon of Amma's early tours and is again becoming popular on prayer flags and T-shirts. The Om-Zia symbol originated from an idea that I had during the pre-tour as we were driving thousands of miles. I wanted an East-meets-West logo to use for some of the publicity that Amma was coming to the West. The "Zia" is a symbol sacred to the Zuni Pueblo Tribe of New Mexico. It represents the sun, giver of life, and each of the four directions has four rays extending out to represent – the four seasons, the four times of day, the four cardinal directions, and the four stages of our life: birth, youth, old age and death. Inside the sun circle Larry Kelley suggested we put the

Sanskrit symbol for "Om" – the original, primordial syllable of creation.

FINDING A HOME FOR M.A.CENTER

The biggest development to come out of the 1988 US Tour was Amma's blessing the Bay Area devotees to search for a location to establish a residential meditation center. For the sake of Amma's children who had to live and work far away from the ashram in India, for the peace and spiritual upliftment of seekers who had come to Amma for guidance, Amma agreed. She asked me to stay behind after the tour had finished in mid-July and help find a suitable location. Amma's primary instruction was that Nature should be considered an important element of the site we chose.

A search committee was formed – Ron Gottsegen, Steve Fleischer, Bhakti Guest and myself – and we began driving around the Bay Area with a realtor. A dozen properties were considered, but the one that stood out right away was a working cattle ranch nestled in the Crow Canyon of San Ramon. First impressions are lasting in many cases; and the image of a dozen sturdy eucalyptus trees 'standing' side by side as you drive onto the property reminded me of a line of devotees holding arati trays to light the path with auspiciousness when Amma arrived at programs throughout India. I felt with absolute confidence that this was the perfect location for the Mata Amritanandamayi Center (M.A.Center) in America. The other three devotees on the search committee felt the same way. We decided to call Amma.

It took some time to describe the property and convey all the details to the monk who was translating. He would call us back. Some time passed and the phone rang. Amma's brief reply could not have been more to the point. If we felt certain about it, then Amma would give her blessing. Period. She also reminded us again that it was for the good of the world, not for Amma's sake, that a center was being established.

That left the small detail of attaining the permit to operate a meditation center in the middle of an agricultural valley. The entire Crow Canyon was protected by the Williamson Act, which allowed for a very narrow set of activities to be conducted on properties bound by this law. Scouting out the neighborhood I noticed there were a lot of ranches, horse stables and nurseries. There was a boy's hostel to help troubled youth nearby, but that was the only example of something outside the purview of ranching or farming.

Meditating one night, an idea came to me. Drawing from my university degree in Environmental Science I thought, "Why not transform the property from a cattle ranch to an organic farm that would showcase sustainable living in an urban area?" It would be a learning center, with a meditation practice at its core. The Green Gulch Zen Center in the Marin Headlands had a similar type of meditation center. The very next morning I called

Lynn Lanier, now known as Brahmacharini Rema Devi, a devotee with a degree from University of California at Berkeley in Landscape Architecture. We collaborated to come up with a master plan for the Crow Canyon property, which could be presented to the Alameda County Board of Supervisors at a public hearing in order to get the permit which was needed. After weeks of meticulous planning, we were ready. I donned a pair of farmer's overalls, dug out an old pair of cowboy boots and a hat and a small group of us proceeded to the hearing. The formal proposal we had written ran about 20 pages and outlined the planting of a fruit orchard, an extensive vegetable garden that could produce income through sales at the local restaurant market, a greenhouse nursery to produce plant starts, an herb-and-flower garden to promote integrated pest management techniques and provide raw materials to craft decorative wreaths that could be sold at holiday time. Beekeeping, product development of fruit jellies and jams, herbal salves and balms, pastoral meditation retreats, free trainings in organic gardening techniques, community service projects were all part of the proposal. At the end of my 30-minute presentation, there was silence. One of the County Supervisors then remarked, "Well then, I think any questions we might have had have already been answered."

The one neighbor who had attended the hearing, perhaps to offer a protest, only requested that the beekeeping be shelved because his horseback riding business might be adversely affected if the bees started attacking the horses or riders. That concession was immediately adopted and the Board of Supervisors unanimously approved the permit to operate M.A.Center at the Crow Canyon location. All in all the deliberations took less than 10 minutes. And so it was that the M.A.Center found its home through the generous donation of a humble devotee, who chose to remain anonymous. The first thing we did was call India to tell Amma the good news.

POINT OF PILGRIMAGE - SAN RAMON ASHRAM

The morning darshan programs would be held on-site, but the evening bhajan programs were still conducted throughout the Bay Area. Within a year we had broken ground on the construction of a proper hall, and Amma would be able to have all the programs on-site. For 25 years now, thousands of people have come to the San Ramon Ashram to receive Amma's blessing and solace in the peaceful surroundings and to offer countless hours of selfless service to support the programs' smooth functioning and humanitarian projects in the Bay Area as well as offering material support to Amma's projects in India. So much so that Amma has declared San Ramon to be a pilgrimage center, a place of holy sanctuary and refuge, due to the tremendous amount of sacrifice and prayer that has been offered there.

The original planting of a modest fruit orchard of some 30 trees has grown to more than 20 acres of edible

Helping get ready for Amma's first visit to San Ramon Ashram, 1988

landscaping, and still expanding. Flower gardens, vegetable gardens, a greenhouse nursery and solar panels have all been set in place. Permaculture workshops have been held to encourage the community to work with nature to bring back the natural harmony on earth. Dozens of service projects have been launched from M.A.Center, with countless devotees benefitting from the spiritual teachings of Amma through the practical application of the service projects, not to mention the recipients of these services themselves.

THE 1988 US TOUR

Everything went smoothly on the tour this year, and there ended up being more than 20 scheduled stops in 1988. Word had spread after last year's visit that Amma was not to be missed if she came back, so more and more people came to meet Amma and receive her blessing. Each person has a special story to tell about how they met Amma. These are stories of life-changing moments, each and every one of them. It was another dream come true for me to see the outpouring of love that was all around.

We were all learning about the path of love from Divine Love herself – Amma is established in that state of Supreme Oneness, and our own love spontaneously ignites in her presence. We had worked hard, thinking of Amma day and night, to bring Amma back in our midst, and she in turn was lighting the lamp of love in our own hearts. The love we feel for Amma was being reflected back to us a thousand-fold. Yes, in the past we all knew of worldly love, the love that is selfish and often heartbreaking. But *prema*, or supreme Love, which is dormant, is awakened when we meet a Great Soul like Amma, and the experience is exhilarating. That is why the experience of meeting a Realized Soul is so transformative. If we can continue to be inspired and take up the spiritual path, we will make tremendous progress staying in their presence. Of course we can do spiritual practices on our own, but they will not bear fruit as quickly. In many cases, without the guidance of a master, we become deluded, thinking that we can guide ourselves to enlightenment or even that we already are enlightened. To have Amma travel so far to meet her children and take their hand while guiding them along the path of love was having a huge impact on their lives. For me, it was bliss to watch those individual transformations take place.

I did a lot of cooking throughout the 1988 tour, especially at the two retreats. Amma herself came to chop vegetables for the evening meal and then proceeded to serve dinner on the second night of the first retreat that was held in the redwood forest of Miranda, much to everyone's delight! It is a favorite tradition that continues to this day at all of Amma's retreats. By now many more devotees were travelling around the country to attend Amma's programs, so there were many more hands to help with the hall set-up and clean-up, although we still had no formal staff to provide consistency throughout. As I was the one to sign the rental agreements for the halls, I was the custodian of the keys and opened the hall before each program. The responsibility fell to me to make sure the hall was properly secured at the end of the evening as well. Some nights, if the darshan program had run late and there was a curfew at the hall, Amma herself would lead the devotees in the tidying up of the hall and the packing up of the bookstall and sound system.

At the close of the 1988 US tour, Amma accepted invitations to lead programs in two new cities, Los Angeles and Maui, in addition to the 15 other cities and towns she was already scheduled to visit for the 1989 tour. In addition to the extensive US Tour itinerary, Amma would fly directly to Europe for the Europe Tour, which now had grown to include London, Paris, and Zurich, in addition to the countries of Germany and Holland.

A BIG CHANGE

A whole year had passed in the twinkling of an eye, and it was 1989. I was spending less and less time in India with Amma as more and more advance planning was needed to co-ordinate Amma's tours. I was fortunate to be with Amma for her first visit to New Delhi and Calcutta though, and have the New Delhi Brahmasthanam Temple consecration as a treasured memory. At the same time as I was being drawn away from India, it was gratifying to see how many Westerners were coming to spend time in India with Amma. Their faces began to shine with the peace that only spiritual practice gives, and seekers from all over the world joined the ashram to become renunciates and lead a life of selfless service with Amma as their Guru. The Divine Mother was connecting with her children; that was clear.

Amma's energy level always seemed to be able to match and surpass whatever was needed in the moment. Travelling with Amma, sitting with her after each program and discussing how everything was going, I constantly marveled at the absolute steadiness of mind Amma had. Nothing could drain her energy level, nothing ruffled her; she was overflowing with energy and awareness. The grueling tour schedule went on in India and abroad, but Amma remained at full strength; it was we, her children, who struggled to keep up! When I look back at the tour schedules, it was back-to-back programs without any rest days from mid-May through mid-July, then off to Europe! If I tried to squeeze in one day off, so that Amma could rest, Amma would notice and go ahead and schedule something in its place.

The world tours were certain to happen each year now, so it became a matter of expanding everything fast enough to include everyone. I needed to double recipes for the retreats now, and the halls got a little bigger. Two more speakers were added to the sound system. A brand-new, heavy-duty 4 X 4 Chevy pick-up truck was donated to transport the tour set-up across the country and back. Amma really wanted me to join her for the Europe tour, and so I finally got a chance to see Amma's programs in Schweibenalpe and Zurich, two places I had shown "A Day With Mother" in 1986.

ONE TOUCH

An interesting moment on the 1989 US Tour happened in the van as I was driving Amma and the group from New York to Boston just after Devi Bhava had finished at St. John the Divine Cathedral in the heart of New York City. It had been an enormous turnout so it was practically sunrise when I put the van in gear and pulled away from the curb. A light drizzle had commenced as I went through the maze of quick turns and construction detours to get us out of the city and onto the correct bridge to head to Boston. It took a lot of concentration, there was no one to guide us, and I had memorized the map of the inner city route so that I would not get lost. It sounded like there was an interesting conversation going on in the back of the van between Amma and the monks, so I asked my co-pilot, Swami Poornamritananda to translate. It seemed one of the monks was asking Amma whether it was necessary to keep on like this, traveling around to the same places year after year. Amma would soon complete this, her third world tour, and wouldn't it be enough to stay in India now? Amma could hold her programs at the ashram in India and now that so many of her spiritual children had finally met her, surely they would come to India. Was it really necessary for Amma to go through such a grueling schedule year after year?

Amma's reply came immediately. Son, if you want to go back and meditate in the ashram, that is fine. But Amma's life is only for this. If Amma touches someone even one time, it changes the course of their life forever. Even if they come to Amma only once, it is enough. It is Amma's sankalpa to embrace as many people as possible in this world. Amma will never stop doing so until her last breath.

A profound silence came over the van; only the sound of the windshield wipers beating out a rhythm was heard. And so it was, with that moving message from Amma, the miles melted away as I drove east for Boston.

AMMA CENTER-NEW HAMPSHIRE

In July of 1989, Amma's tour was wrapping up on the East Coast at Jani and Ganganath McGill's healing center in Temple, New Hampshire, which would soon become 'Amma Center-New Hampshire.'

Jani had such a lovely connection from the very moment she met Amma in 1987, and has always been helping with the US Tour since that time up to the present day. Their family did whatever needed to be done, whether that meant hosting the first East Coast retreat at their healing center or cleaning out their rustic barn for weeks on end before Amma arrived so that the Devi Bhava Darshan could be held there.

I also believe that the McGill family was extremely blessed to be the only devotees in the world to have ever celebrated Guru Purnima with Amma in their home's spacious meditation room. As the auspicious full moon day happened to occur just as the US Tour had ended, but before Amma departed for Europe, they had the honor to host a handful of devotees who gathered to celebrate the day most sacred to a disciple.

As it turned out, another big moment took place in their home. The US Tour had ended and everyone was busy preparing to fly to Europe the next day. Amma was giving me instructions regarding the coming year's tour, since I would be staying behind to do the preliminary organizing for 1990 before returning to the ashram in India. This is when Amma would approve any new cities to be added to the next year's schedule, and would always give me some new ideas.

NEW IDEAS...

This year was no different, but no one could have guessed what our beloved Amma had in mind! She instructed me to travel to new places, but not cities this time — countries! I should go to Canada, Japan and Australia to arrange the first-ever programs there. Amma said her children in those places were longing for her, and it was time for Amma to go there to meet them. I thought to myself, "OK, but we don't know anyone from any of those countries." But I nodded my agreement without hesitation. Amma's first world tour had come about this way; my experience was that with Amma's blessing, anything is possible. No need for too much talking, Amma would show the way ahead.

The US Tour planning for 1990 was going on smoothly with only one new city, Dallas, added in. The big change was to host five retreats over the course of the tour next year — in Maui, Los Angeles, San Ramon, Seattle and Temple, New Hampshire. With no fixed staff, no cell phones, no laptop computers, the help of so many ardent devotees in each city was crucial to pull everything together for the summer tour. I spent most of my time coordinating with each of the nine regional areas, travelling there to help with finding the right facilities, cooking a benefit dinner and meeting with the families who would host Amma and the monks. This year the retreats would involve a lot of cooking, and as I was the lead cook, my lists had to be put in with a lot of accuracy now, because come tour time, I was busy with other details. By the middle of September I had most of my traveling finished up and was satisfied with where things stood for the U.S. portion of the tour.

Canada was already coming together smoothly after I had gone up to meet with a family from Vancouver who had met Amma in Seattle in May. They were elated to hear the news that next year's tour would include Vancouver, and that they could host Amma and the group in their home. They immediately began to plan for Amma's program and had other family friends who were interested to help. All the makings for a great program in Vancouver were coming together, and now I could turn my attention where it was really needed.

RUBIK'S CUBES

That autumn in San Ramon the greater part of my mind was on Japan and Australia. I wanted Amma to do those programs en route to America to save money on airfare. The same 10-city, 'around-the-world' airline ticket was still available at a good price, with a slight surcharge for going as far south as Australia. That would make it possible to bring Amma there. That meant they would have to be scheduled at the beginning of the tour in May. That didn't leave a lot of time to spare, as I was hoping to spend a few months in India with Amma. That left me about three months to plan for two new countries.

Amma had given me two new Rubik's Cubes, and their names were Australia and Japan. I had only one address from Australia; it was for a lady by the name of Patricia Witts of Sydney, who had come to meet Amma in Kerala this past year. In the case of Japan, we did not have even a single contact. Writing a letter of introduction to Patricia Witts was straightforward, easy even. I introduced myself and let her know that Amma would be coming to Australia next May. I would be visiting Sydney just after the New Year to arrange Amma's visit. Could I possibly meet up with her then and do a video showing or two in Sydney? Would she like to help with that? "Oh yes, that would be lovely," Patricia wrote back. That was enough of a lead for me to relax about Australia for the time being. Once I got myself there, Amma's grace would flow, as ever.

Japan was an entirely different story. I began by writing to a few different meditation centers and philosophical groups I could find listed in the back of various books I pored over at the Shambala Bookstore on Telegraph Avenue in Berkeley. I even wrote to the 'One Straw Revolution' founder, an organic farmer with spiritual ideas about Mother Nature hoping for any glimmer of response. I got none. On a long shot, I drove into San Francisco, where I explored the Japantown district. Walking up and down the streets, popping into small shops and cafes, reading posters on the signboards, just putting myself in the flow of Japantown, I finally met one person interested in meditation in an obscure bookshop. We talked about Amma, and I told him about her upcoming program being planned for Japan. Did he know anyone who might be interested? Was he interested? Yes, yes, he replied. We drove back to the San Ramon Ashram so he could watch Amma's video and learn more about the proposed visit to Japan. He was very touched and straight away made some phone calls to Japan to try to find a contact for me. He made so much effort, but to no avail. There was not much more he could do; it had been a long time since he had lived there. But what he did give me were a few addresses in Tokyo of people he knew. He said that I could write to them and try that way. It wasn't much, but it was all I had to go on.

So I did. I wrote a total of five letters. It was early December of 1989. Each day I would check the M.A.Center mail for any reply from Japan. Nothing. I knew time was running out. My ticket to Tokyo was booked for January 9th. From there I would fly to Australia to meet Patricia on January 18th. On the 27th I would leave for Malaysia to try for a program venue there, then back home to Amma by February 8th to join Amma's North India Tour. I was really hoping that I had left myself enough time.

The New Year was ushered in, and that was it. Nothing. I would have to depart for Tokyo empty-handed in the total dead of winter. Five years earlier I had come to the US to arrange for Amma's first visit, but I had family and friends to rely on. A feeling of intense detachment came over me. I was out of ideas, there was nothing left to do but pack my small travel bag and pray. I shed tears for Japan.

SAN RAMON ASHRAM

January 7th 1990

Glorious, glorious day! A letter from Japan had arrived! It was from a young Japanese woman by the name of Masako Watanabe of Tokyo. It was a simple letter with a funny plastic credit card tucked inside. She wrote:

Dear Kusuma,
I received your letter and it sounds interesting what you are doing. I enclose a pre-paid phone card so you can call me from Narita Airport when you arrive.
Sincerely,
Masako Watanabe

That was enough for me to go on. Strangely, I felt it was confirmed that Amma's Japan program was on, just with the receipt of that simple letter. Only one person was needed in a city (or country!) for Amma's pure grace to flow; Patricia in Australia and Masako in Japan. I had never seen a phone card before. All I could do was stare at it with wonder and thank Amma for working in such extraordinary ways. My heart felt certain that all was on track.

TOKYO

And so it was. I called Masako two days later when I arrived and she came from Shinjuko suburb to bring me to stay in her tiny, 15-tatami-mat apartment in the middle of sprawling Tokyo while I organized Amma's first visit to Japan. Her English was flawless and we hit it off right away. She had been an exchange student in America during high school which, ironically, is why she had sent me the phone card. She had wanted to spend time practicing American English with someone who had written such an unusual letter! Little did she know that she was destined to be Amma's first translator in Tokyo and would work side by side with Koizumi-san of the Tokyo Women's College to be the co-host for Amma's first Japan program, May 18-20, 1990.

The following year, Brandon Smith (now Brahmachari Shantamrita) was sent by Amma to organize her second visit to Japan. Since then, he has continued to serve Amma at her center in Japan and at other locations around the world.

SYDNEY AND MELBOURNE

Arriving in Sydney was a relief. It felt like anything was possible after breaking through so many barriers in Japan. Patricia Witts was a very nice middle-aged mum with three grown children in high school and the trades. We had a splendid video showing in her home in Chatsworth and another nearby venue. Then, with quiet, practical enthusiasm, she warmed up to the idea of filling the role of first Sydney hostess for Amma hearing what the true need was. After all, she had visited Amma in her home in Kerala, so why shouldn't she return Amma the same hospitality, she thought. There was not any time to waste, so we drove around to find halls in the Chatsworth area nearby the Witts family home where Amma would stay.

Patricia had also connected with some contacts in Melbourne, and so we booked a bus for me to go south and do the same video show there. A charming, mature group of spiritual seekers who had already spent many years meditating, attending satsang and making pilgrimage with various teachers from India met me in Melbourne and hosted a video showing there. James Conquest, Eugenie Maheswari Knox and Campbell McKellar were all there that night and continue their service to host Amma at the M.A. Centre in Melbourne. After spending 10 action packed days finding halls, showing the videos, having meetings, and sharing lists from the US Tour, everyone in Australia who I had met was ready to do whatever was needed to host Amma's program in May. So when it was time for me to fly back to India, it felt like all was on course for a robust Amma in Australia tour to come together in May.

CHAPTER NINE

The Fall of 1990

Tarangayita apime sangat samudrayanti

Though they (negative tendencies) rise only as ripples in the beginning, they become like an ocean.

Narada Bhakti Sutras, Verse 45

I had been touring nonstop for five years to arrange Amma's programs around the world. My service had become my only sadhana and the beautiful balance of my early years with Amma had been eroded by my lack of shraddha; meditation, satsang and self-study had fallen away like so many dry leaves on a withered branch. On top of that, I had let go of my yoga practice and study of Sanskrit to the point where their place in my life was non-existent. I was busy doing service. *Living and breathing in Amma all the time, no need to worry,* I egotistically thought, and carelessly let go of the core of my practice.

That was when random negative thoughts began to disturb me. In the beginning, they would just drift through my mind like the needling, humming drone of a mosquito. Underestimating their cumulative power, I just ignored them, brushing them away to the dark recesses of my mind. But they kept coming back. Suddenly I could see faults in everyone around me. I found one person irritating, someone else was lazy, or a volunteer would show up late and I would get stressed out. The young woman who eventually left the organization, the same one who I had to be careful of because of her jealousy, seemed so hypocritical to me, allowing people to fawn over her to get access to Amma, and then cutting them down behind their backs. Even though she was so loved and revered, she would manipulate situations and was very controlling. All these things built up and made me angry.

These seemingly insignificant thoughts and situations began to slowly accumulate and poison my perspective. That's how it is with negative thoughts: if we pay no heed to them, they slowly lull us into a state of complacency; they become a negative state of mind. Pretty soon our entire perception is filtered through that negative mind set. Before we know it, we become trapped in our own whirlpool of negativity, sucked into its vortex, careening from one bad choice to another. Inevitably we end up drowning in the non-negotiable consequences of our choices.

As Sri Krishna unmistakably warns Arjuna in verses 62-63 of the second discourse of the Bhagavad Gita:

Dhyayato visayanpumsah sangastesupajayate
Sangatsanjayate kamah kamat krodho'bhijayate

Dwelling on sense objects, attachment arises.

From attachment, desire is born, from desire anger arises.

Krodhad bhavati sammohah sammohat smrti vibhramah
Smrti bhrams'ad buddhinas'o buddhin asat pranas'yati

From anger comes delusion; from delusion, memory is lost, from the loss of memory, discrimination is destroyed; from the destruction of discrimination, one perishes.

The year of 1990 found me deep in a quagmire of my own making. Emotionally drained by my negative thinking, weighed down by not getting those thoughts off my chest, physically tired from constant traveling, spiritually dried up from lack of spiritual practice, I didn't see the danger I was in. I didn't make the effort to reach out to any of my spiritual elders who had been so dear to me, who had always been there for me through thick and thin. Worst of all, I didn't even confide in Amma. Instead, a foolish sense of pride that others should not know about the turmoil in my mind led me to a dangerous crossroad without my even knowing it. In a word, my ego, which I had set out to transcend, had instead become my closest confidante.

The more closed off my heart became, the more I isolated myself from Amma. My brooding had taken on a life of its own and soon a year had passed in self-inflicted misery and internal conflict. Others were enjoying the best of times; programs were spreading around the world — America, Canada, Europe, Australia, Singapore and Japan had opened their hearts and arms to Amma. But poor me, just curled up in a little ball feeling sorry for myself.

Looking back, I know that others watched that year pass painfully for me. Some told me later that I had been unapproachable; no one could get through the wall I had erected. I wasn't listening to anything, not letting anyone in, not even Amma. Finally, in my weakened state, desire reared its ugly head and swallowed me whole. It chewed me up and spit me out to land on the other side, far away from Amma.

Disconcerting dreams swooped in, fantasies of the perfect relationship, the perfect life, anything to escape the irony I was caught in: I had everything I had ever prayed for, I was serving Amma to the utmost, but I had lost my desire to reach the goal. Everything felt flat, contradictory. I had lost my humility, my balance, my aim. My headstrong nature plunged me into a series of ill-fated decisions that still reverberate through my life, though now I can finally see the deep harmony underlying them all. That part came later, though. Much later.

Now I entered the blame-game phase. Basically, I started subtly blaming others for what I was experiencing. When we begin to externalize our inner process by targeting others as the source of our misery, we have reached the height of delusion. It's the "poor me" syndrome on steroids, bringing us down faster than a hurricane settling on the coast of New Orleans. It is a brutal, ruthless state of mind that spares no one, ultimately not even oneself. The destruction wrought by forgetting the truth, *tat tvam asi*, "You are That," is devastating. Every bearing and measure of our spiritual life is thrown off-kilter. We embrace what we should reject, and reject what we most need.

Take anger, resentment, unbridled ego and self-righteousness, mix in a little bit of self-absorbed pity and a big dab of stubbornness... and you have a recipe for disaster. What began as insignificant little things such as getting my feelings hurt, feeling misunderstood and unappreciated, being crabby and short-tempered with people, or judging them for being mean-spirited and dishonest, piled up. And then, like Gulliver's Lilliputians who eventually overwhelmed him, they toppled me over completely.

Only years later did I see how skewed my perception had become. Instead of looking within myself for flaws, I was too busy finding fault with others. I had not understood why Amma tolerates such behavior around her. Later I saw that it is not because she agrees with it, but because it acts like a rock tumbler, each one's sharp points getting worn down by the other's rough edges. That is often the case when living in community. I needed to learn the lesson of not criticizing others, when I myself was struggling to root out my own bad qualities. I could have more effectively kept my eye on the Guru, and not have allowed the negative qualities of someone who appeared to be close to Amma spoil my view. Blaming others for problems created by my own willfulness, arrogance and anger was easier than introspection. These patterns of blame and projection, combined with the hostility which had been brewing within me for a year, created the perfect storm.

Sometimes we lack the maturity to learn our spiritual lessons in a gracious, gentle manner and this certainly was the case with me. In September 1990, having completed all the preliminary planning for the 1991 US Tour, I left the itinerary and organizing plans sitting on top of my desk at the San Ramon ashram. In a three-ring binder, I also carefully arranged all the regional area contacts for around the world, including my meticulous notes spanning five years for tour planning, retreat planning, recipes, etc. and kept it on my desk along with the 1991 US Tour master plan. I had no intention of letting Amma's tours fall apart, just because I was. On my way out of the office, I said to one of the residents working nearby, "There's something on my desk you're going to need." After taking proper leave of the monk in charge, saying that I needed to 'take a break,' I packed my sister's car with my few belongings and drove away.

With that, I left Amma, not saying much of anything at all to the one who had mattered most in my life, who had given me all that I needed. It was an audacious, in-auspicious close to a glorious phase of my life.

DEAR DIARY...

The first significant thing I did after leaving the San Ramon ashram was to write in my diary noting down what I thought had gone wrong. I had driven to the Mendocino coast in Northern California. I remember watching the tide slowly back up into the estuary at Point Mendocino, forming a soothing backdrop for catching my breath. The salt water mixed with freshwater and brought a bounty of diversity to life there. I passed my thirtieth birthday on the river, and then I drove east, back to New Mexico, where it had all begun. I was able to find a job in a restaurant and a place to live. My diary was tucked away somewhere, soon to be misplaced and forgotten.

I got a boyfriend. The relationship ended up a disaster. I buried away my most special memories. I made no effort to contact Amma and seek her counsel; I didn't attend the satsang group that met in nearby Santa Fe. In a way, I stopped communicating with my own heart. I built a fortress in my head to keep all of my self-recriminating thoughts at bay, so that I could do what I wanted. And, really, what did I want? An onlooker could have been forgiven for thinking that I was hell-bent on making a mess of my life. I lived those months like nothing mattered anymore. The modern age of cynicism was the perfect stage for my self-absorbed, petulant self. No one could tell me anything, and I didn't want to hear it anyway.

Though it was a self-imposed time-out, oddly enough I still chanted my mantra as if part of me could see my spiritual life unraveling and refused to completely let go. Perhaps it was a subconscious fear that I would forget my mantra and never find my way back to Amma. Even though I was in the process of trashing my life, deep inside, like a faint pulse, I still felt love for Amma and hoped that she would forgive me and save me. Somehow, a year slid by.

It was spring cleaning time the following year in 1992 when I came across my journal from the day I had left. I sat down to read it and was shocked: the essence of nearly every complaint boiled down to my blaming someone else! Many of the situations I had suffered in I had set in motion by my own actions, my own misperceptions. In that moment, I could see the truth so clearly. Suddenly it was hard to take a breath and tears began streaming down my face. Disgusted with myself, I sat there, stunned, for the longest time.

Then I decided something. So fierce and strong was the urge, I walked out onto the Taos Mesa and collected armfuls of dried sagebrush, carefully dug a pit and lit a fire. It blazed up all at once, as sage does, and I burned my diary there and then. I made a strong determination, a vow in fact, to get real with myself. I would write a list, a different list. This one would not be about other people, but about myself. That night I realized that happiness is a choice, not a gift someone else gives us. And I realized that true healing happens only when we stop blaming and start forgiving others and ourselves.

Looking back, it seems as if it should have been only a few short stepping stones from that day of discovery back into Amma's arms, but Pandora's box has a funny way of not wanting to be shut after being thrown open. As spiritual seekers — as human beings — we are a strange admixture of free will and destiny, the former not easily exerted, the latter not easily manipulated. If we willfully choose to carve out our own path, we can be sure that the universe will arrange for more than a few karmic years before the arc bends back to where we want it.

So at this point, I started really crying. From the depths of my soul, I cried for Amma to save me, to fish me out of the muddy puddle into which I had hurled myself. To give me the strength of conviction to return. To not forget that it is never too late to come back to spiritual life. I had suffered enough to know that the spiritual truths Amma was teaching were authentic. Nobody could ever love me with such a pure love as Amma. Her grace was the stuff of legends. How could I have succumbed to amnesia when it came to witnessing Amma heal Dattan, the leper? How could I have been so mesmerized by *maya* – the illusion of reality, the glittering ephemera of the world?

I mustered up my courage and decided it was time to go and face the music, literally. So I promised myself to attend an evening bhajan program sometime during the US Tour that summer. To be honest, I was nervous and afraid to go see Amma. How would she react? What might all the others have to say? What if it was awful? Although all this internal banter was going on, frankly, at this point, I was more scared to stay away!

As it happened, I was visiting Berkeley for a 10-year class reunion when the urge to see Amma became irresistible. I had been telling some old college friends about my time with Amma, and as none of them had met her before, it was a pretty safe audience for me to share my reminiscences with — until one friend said, "Hey, Amma is in town. Let's go to a program!" My stomach did a couple of flips and some butterflies fluttered in there too. Was I ready? Was it that simple? Just go to a program? Go see Amma! Just as hundreds of other people were doing that same night, off we went.

BERKELEY 1992

Kannunir kondu nin padam kazhurkam
katyayani ni kaivitalle...

With my tears I will wash your Feet, O Katyayani
But please, do not forsake me...

Amritanjali, Volume One

As it happened, the program venue was near the University of California's Berkeley campus, my old stomping ground, a place where I had arranged countless programs for Amma. In theory I might have been quite relaxed. But I wasn't. Walking in the door to the hall, I was completely nervous. And the first two people I saw in the distance walking in my direction were my two favorites: Swamiji and Brahmacharini Nirmalamrita, my old friend from the first video showing in 1986. It's hard to believe it, but I ran back out of the hall with my tail between my legs. I was ready to see Amma, but not my dear brothers and sisters. I was so anxious about how they would react. Can you imagine the surprise on my college friend's face when she turned and saw that she was alone? Catching up with me, she said, "What's wrong with you? I thought you wanted to come see Amma. Why did you run outside?"

I made some lame excuse and we left, although she was a bit peeved since we had driven through a lot of traffic to reach the program on time, only to turn around and leave.

That night I took inventory of my inner state. Maybe I wasn't as ready to see Amma as I had thought. Why such a strong emotional reaction to my former spiritual friends? I concluded that more preparation, more self-reflection was needed before I could go to Amma. But I did not get off so easily. The next day, late in the afternoon, my friend dropped by and basically told me that we were going to an Amma program whether I liked it or not. She didn't want to hear another word about it, so I might as well get in the car. Driving there, I was chanting my mantra like crazy. Now things were really taking an unexpected turn, totally out of my control. There was nothing I could do but surrender. Walking into the hall this time was easier. I just imagined an invisibility cloak around myself and let my friend lead me into the hall to sit wherever she picked. I kept my eyes averted so I wouldn't lose my nerve.

The bhajans were incredible; they soothed me like I had never been soothed before. Before long, I felt a sense of blissful, welcome relaxation and could take my first breath again. As the last note of the arati faded and the closing prayers were chanted, I felt a gentle hand on my shoulder. It was another of my favorite friends, Brahmacharini Rema Devi of San Ramon, looking like an angel with a huge smile on her face. She took my hand and led me through all the people right up to Amma.

I will never forget that moment. It felt as if everyone in the room had stopped breathing at the same time. Amma looked up, our eyes locked and we both burst into tears. Amma pulled me down into her lap and then held me in the most loving embrace for a very long time. She released me and we gazed into each other's eyes again. Then we laughed out loud and cried a bit more. Swamiji and Swami Paramatmananda, Ron, Steve Fleischer and Bhakti had all come close to Amma's chair. Everyone was beaming so much love at me that I couldn't even think. It was like swimming in a pot overflowing with divine love in every direction.

My friend was taken aback by the emotion of it all. Later that night when we were leaving the hall, she said, "I have never seen so much love in my life. Those people love you so much. You are really lucky. You are really special to them." I had no words. I was so entirely humbled by the experience that layer after layer of my fortress of ego crumbled.

Though the distance measured in miles and years remained many before I would finally return to live in Amritapuri, and though I have made many more mistakes in my unfolding path with Amma, I can truly say that from that point onward, I was never again "away from Amma" in my heart. Since being reunited that night in Berkeley, though I have struggled still, in entirely different ways, I have been profoundly joyful and deeply nourished by my connection with the ancient Divine Mother who is Mata Amritananadamayi. And for the light of that pure grace to have shone on me again, I am eternally grateful.

CHAPTER 10

Measuring the Ocean

How do we measure the ocean? Can we explain its mystery? Its breadth, its depth? The countless life forms taking shelter in its vastness? It is not possible with the instruments we have to accomplish such a gargantuan task. It is enough to describe the ocean as best we can: its saltiness, its mysterious, moon-driven tidal surges, and all the rest. We can test the water with our big toe, we can go on describing and debating all its aspects, but finally each one of us must decide. Do I want to see for myself what it is to dive into the sea? Do I want to get wet? Do I want to learn to swim?

It makes no difference to the ocean if one more person jumps in and discovers its wonders, or if one person gets out, frustrated and disheartened. Millions may swim, sail or fish in a given day. The ocean is not bothered. It is not changed by the fact that some swim and some do not. It is there for all, to whatever extent we avail ourselves of it. The ocean will go on as it has since the beginning of time.

The same can be said of the Guru. Who can fathom the fullness of the Guru's Realization? Who can describe it? Except through our own limited powers of observation and discernment, there is no definitive litmus test to prove a Guru's enlightenment. But finally, as in the case of the ocean, to perfectly quantify the Guru's realized state in order to measure it is not the point. It is for us to decide what direction to aim for with our own fleeting life.

What is it that draws some of us to spiritual life and not others? Why do some people decide to seek a spiritual guide, and others are repelled by the very suggestion? There are many aspects to answering that question fairly: many obvious reasons, some more hidden. However, most people, rich and poor alike, could agree that there is an emptiness, an aching, a thread of sorrow that runs through our lives that leaves us wanting more, longing to find some deeper meaning in it all. Some might turn to spiritual books, lectures or teachers to try and get some answers, some peace, some happiness. Others lose themselves to drugs, alcohol, or bad relationships to dull their pain. Many fall into a depression over the state of their lives and the world, unable to live with this hollow ache that cannot be understood. Multitudes of people the world over muddle along, more or less content with the status quo, and live out the events of their lives, swinging like a pendulum between happiness and sorrow. Each one of us develops a unique approach to living life whether we are conscious of it or not.

Suppose we are of the first group mentioned, and become inspired by what we read, hear or see in a Guru; we might go a little farther. We might consider spending some time learning to meditate, trying some hatha yoga, or attending a spiritual retreat. We find solace and understanding when we turn to spirituality. If we are fortunate,

we meet a True Master like Amma. At that moment, our soul knows that it has arrived in the presence of a great soul, a *Mahatma*. At that moment, the struggle between the soul and the ego begins, the tussle between our spiritual destiny and our free will is set in motion, and life becomes a dynamic tension between self-discovery and self-delusion. Meeting a Realized Master is the catalyst to hasten the awakening. I now believe that once we meet a Mahatma there is no turning back from the journey; it is merely a question of how fast we want to go. For some it is a long, combative journey, full of missteps and diversions, while others enjoy a quick smooth ride. We are the determining factor. The Great Soul abides patiently in her awakened state; if we choose to come or go, it is not of any consequence to the Master. We are the ones with something to gain, not the other way around.

There is a tradition, an ancient one, which continues unbroken to this day — the path to Self-Realization, when a seeker establishes a bond with a Guru who can take us beyond the cycle of birth and death to Liberation. There is a vast body of spiritual writing, both ancient and contemporary — the Upanishads, the Puranas, the Bhagavad-Gita, and commentaries on these, which elucidates every aspect and detail of the Guru-disciple relationship and what the spiritual path entails. This written record is not someone's imagination or conjecture; it is written from the direct experience of those who have gone before us and reached the pinnacle of human consciousness, the liberated state of pure Oneness.

The Guru's commitment to the disciple is absolute, unfailing. The Guru will teach in such a way that the ego and selfish desires will be transformed. That is the only goal of the teacher — to awaken the student. Countless are the souls who have walked this path, sought out spiritual Masters, and done whatever they had to do to merge their egocentric consciousness into the great Oneness, ultimately victorious. But it is not for the faint-hearted; it takes a strong mind to tread the path and keep going further and further into the mystery of existence. There are many more who have failed than who have succeeded, especially in the age of cynicism we are mired in today.

We must scrutinize a Guru before we surrender to them. We must be fully satisfied with their ability to guide us, but once we make our decision to accept a Master and follow the path to the goal, we should not go on scrutinizing or the Guru will not be able to guide us to Self-Realization.

HONEYMOON

I rejoined Amma for the US tour in 1993; she welcomed me back with open arms. The programs had grown in size and there was a staff van now. I was graciously included. Though it was difficult to confront all that I had left behind, as the tour moved across the country, old friends greeted me and we cried and laughed together over the self-created follies of our lives.

At the end of the 1993 US Tour I regrouped in New Mexico and then arranged to go back to be with Amma in India. I was longing for my spiritual life again; I didn't want to miss my chance. Amma was so forgiving and encouraging in every way. One of the first things she said to me just after I arrived when we were sitting in her room was that the past was a cancelled check. I had to let it be that, and not dwell on the past. Otherwise I would not make any progress. Amma didn't blame me at all; she kept me close beside her, though there were so many more people now vying for her attention.

Everyone was happy to see me; Amma's father Sugunanandan Acchan cried when he first laid eyes on me. His broad smile said it all and he shook his head in the most loving way, and said, "Kusumam, Kusumam," in a tone laden with tenderness. All the elders of the community, many now wearing the yellow robes of formal initiation, let me know in their own quiet, gentle way that they were glad to see me back. There were many new residents who didn't even know me, and it felt good to do seva with them, anonymously so to speak.

Yet, it was difficult to find my old rhythm, my balance, my practice. I realized how easy it is to tear something down, but rebuilding is a far greater task. I winced when I saw how much damage had been done to my former enthusiasm for the goal. So I decided to go back to the basics, to try and regain my lost innocence. Amma was always encouraging us to have a beginner's mind. Was it really possible?

To follow the path of love, it is necessary to love the path first! The biggest obstacle I found was my inability to forgive myself and believe in myself again. So I decided to start there. The devotional practices that I had cast aside so carelessly, I now returned to in order to transform my thoughts, actions and speech into peace and tranquility once again. I had always enjoyed repeating my mantra and contemplating the face of the Divine Mother, my beloved Amma. I had always felt so much fulfillment when offering my energy, talent and intellect to selflessly serving others. My heart melted hearing the devotional singing of Amma calling me to higher ground. My prayers became heartfelt again — *Please Amma, save me, guide me back to grace!*

Slowly but surely, my memory of the Truth returned. My spiritual amnesia subsided; my discernment for keeping good company got reestablished. I could see some of what my attachments were and sit with that awareness, trying to witness the play of emotions within me, instead of being caught up in it.

Only one time during this period did someone say something negative that really affected me. She waited for an opportunity to approach when I was alone and then said, "Why did you bother to come back? Why not just enjoy your life and leave all this behind once and for all?" I was too shocked to reply. She was known for her deep devotion to Amma, but at the same time could be really not nice behind the scenes. Ironically, it was the same woman who ended up leaving the ashram herself. I made a mental note to keep my distance from her, though many times there was no way around it.

She put me in charge of assigning volunteer work at the seva desk, and right away I was back in the frying pan. Externally I was managing; being the seva coordinator was easy compared to being the tour organizer, but internally I was struggling. Putting the pieces of spiritual life back together takes time and fortitude. I could now see that the initial splashes and paddling around after diving into spiritual life were wonderful, buoyant moments. But as we progress along the path, there are many hard lessons to learn and painful experiences to go through. We should probably be less surprised by this. To become a medical doctor or earn a PhD, how much effort and sacrifice have to be made? Spirituality is no less exacting a path than an academic subject, after all. However, a bigger question loomed – Was I up to the task?

I quickly saw that it was up to me to keep my spirits up, to learn my lessons well and change. If I could not maintain enthusiasm for reaching the goal, then the pure grace that flows around Amma like the torrential, unending flow of Niagara Falls would be to no avail. Grace is ours for the taking in equal measure to the effort we make. There is no lack on the part of a True Master like Amma; it is more often the faltering footsteps of the disciple discerned on the path.

MEASURING MY COMMITMENT

One of my best friends, Nancy Crawford, then known as Suneeti and later as Brahmacharini Nirmalamrita, had moved to India and become a renunciate at the ashram.

We had worked together on all the tours starting in 1986, especially on planning the retreats. Suneeti had been a research scientist at the University of California, Berkeley, in the same College of Natural Resources I had graduated from, and we had a lot in common. We had always enjoyed great conversations about spirituality, life and death, whenever we had a spare moment. Though she had many friends, I had been a big sister to her in her early years with Amma and was someone she would confide in. Now the tables were turned and I looked to her steadiness and strong determination as an inspiration.

While getting to know her during the US tours, I knew that she had suffered from cancer, not once, but twice. She had an intriguing viewpoint about it. Both times she had gone the traditional allopathic route with full chemotherapy, full radiation, full suffering, full recovery. But she said that changing her mindset and lifestyle is what really made the difference. The second bout with cancer is what had brought her to spirituality.

Suneeti had a clear mind about death. She knew what cancer felt like in her body, and was not at all naïve about it. The possibility of getting it a third time was very real; she still went for an annual checkup to make sure that she was continuing in good health, cancer-free. She did not think she could survive a third time. What that would mean was not something she dwelled on, but accepted with an unperturbed mind.

Early on after my return, we had a powerful conversation on this very point. She told me her most cherished wish was to serve Amma with her last breath and enjoy the life of renunciation to its fullest. She said if she ever got cancer again she would rather stay near Amma and serve Amma up to the very last moment of her life. She had already thought it through. It felt as though she was cutting a deal, an unspoken one, such that if she sensed she had cancer growing in her body again, she would let it take its course, she would not waste money on an expensive, futile treatment. If she interrupted her spiritual life for a third round of chemo and radiation, it would surely weaken her to the extent that she could not continue on her chosen path with Amma. Even with treatment, she knew she probably would not survive a third relapse. I drew a lot of inspiration from her now, as she had drawn from me in the past — her commitment to the spiritual path with Amma was unwavering.

One afternoon, sitting in Suneeti's room on the balcony level of the Kali Temple, I asked her candidly. If it happened a third time and she had to pick between a long, debilitating treatment with an uncertain outcome or just living life out on her own terms for as long as possible, knowing that something was going on in her body, which would be her choice? Without a moment's hesitation she said she would pick the second option. Continuing with a thoughtful smile, she explained to me that the new lease on life she had been given when she met Amma and moved to India was everything. She loved God so much, she wanted to serve her Guru and serve others with whatever time she had. She did not think she could survive a third round of cancer. She did not want to ruin any time she might have with Amma because the long drawn-out treatments would be so incapacitating. She did not want that to be her condition when she said goodbye to Amma. After our conversation was over, I had to ask myself, did I have that kind of dedication and clarity?

ASHRAM LIFE IN THE 1990'S

The first Western families had joined the ashram and it was delightful to see the children running and playing with Amma every chance they got. There was Priya and Krishna Unni from Los Angeles; Sarada and Manju from Canada; Gopi, Sudha and Gemma from Seattle; Aparna and Manohari of New Mexico; Santosh of Austria; and Sridevi and Anandi of Germany. These families were pioneers of sorts, managing to raise their children, do their selfless service, and dedicate their lives to spirituality all within the setting of the monastery. These kids' childhoods were blessed in extraordinary ways by growing up in Amma's divine presence.

The Western Office was officially set up to welcome and accommodate the steady stream of international visitors; I was asked to help there and lead the orientations. A Western food canteen had been started and there were devotees arriving from all over the world to fill it! Ram's Bazaar, a flea market and second-hand store, was set up to benefit the orphanage. People from all corners of the world chose to become lifelong residents at that time and there was an infusion of eagerness to learn about spiritual life on the part of the new Western residents.

Amma is the most approachable and accessible Guru in the world, answering each one with a specific instruction of how to proceed in their spiritual life. This practice continues to this day, with Amma spending countless hours in the darshan hall meeting each person for an embrace and counsel, or next to the Arabian Sea for meditation and satsang. Amma has never sat apart from the spiritual community that has formed around her, she is part and parcel of it, always in the middle of the beehive directing the ashram activities, conducting important meetings and discussions out in the open for all to see and hear. Anyone can come close to Amma for a hug, and linger nearby for as much time as they need to soothe their soul. Anyone can directly ask Amma a question, or bring their problems to her. There is no personal secretary who intermediates between the devotees and Amma. How uplifting that somewhere in the world there is still to be found purity and unconditional love!

LEAVING AGAIN

Amma included me on all of the tours in India and abroad. She even asked me to run the sound system on the tour of Mauritius and Reunion Island in the spring of 1994. The problem was that I couldn't recapture my former drive for the goal. I had to re-create my world with Amma anew, and it was not going well because of my attachments to the past.

The unconscious expectations I had had when resuming my life with Amma in India were not being met, but how could they have been? The access to Amma I had enjoyed in the early days was blocked. The seva coordinating was my excuse for not keeping a strict timetable for sadhana. I began comparing myself to others and feeling that I was sincere and they were hypocrites. My introspection had become superficial, not incisive. A very dangerous current I began to swim in.

That is the nature of expectations, self-righteousness and judgment; they are the preamble to discontent. It took several years of effort before I could admit this to myself, but eventually I had to face it — I didn't love the sadhana anymore, everything felt flat and dreary. I felt deeply disappointed with myself that my inspiration to follow the path had dried up.

Everywhere around me were examples of dedication and selflessness, but my life felt as if it was an empty shell of what had been. All the promise and intensity of my early years with Amma had evaporated. Discouragement and restlessness went on increasing. People started getting on my nerves again, I sat apart from those whom I could just as easily have turned to for satsang. Internally I was adrift again, but kept myself busy with *seva*, ignoring the warning signs, and increasingly keeping a distance from Amma. Danger, danger, danger encircling me all around.

One of the biggest pitfalls on the spiritual path is when we let our mind start to blame others. When we allow our focus to drift away from the goal and fix on something negative that someone else is doing, we are lost. This bad habit is the antithesis of spiritual life; it is the same as eating a low dose of poison every day until enough accumulates and we perish.

Why blame the teacher for the lack of commitment on the part of the student? Why was the Guru chosen in the first place? Because we felt confident in their ability to guide us, and because we wanted to be guided! As the student, it was my responsibility to approach Amma with my doubts, but again, I was a coward. In 1996, I packed my bag and left, this time for good.

CHAPTER ELEVEN

Never Too Late

MAKING SENSE OF LEAVING

The mind is a funny thing. Ultimately, there is no rationale that can adequately explain why it leads us someplace other than where we thought we were going. There is no convenient, tidy explanation for why I left Amma. It was the accumulation of a lot of things gone wrong – when we lose our focus and stillness of mind, anything is possible. Still struggling to understand my departure from Amma the first time, how could I make sense of leaving Amma twice?

Call it karma, selfishness, the powerful delusion of maya, or the blood-stained field of Kurukshetra where Lord Krishna sang out the Bhagavad Gita to Arjuna; the quicksand of negativity is very difficult to extricate oneself from.

When I think back on it after all these years, the image of an atom comes to my mind. In the center of an atom lies the nucleus. The electrons are organized in different concentric shells or orbitals spinning around the nucleus. If Amma were the nucleus, then in 1983-1990, I was

one of the electrons spinning in a tight orbit of the shell closest to the nucleus. There is a tremendous binding energy exerted on the electron to orbit in that shell. Now imagine an electron starting to wobble, or having a slight variance in its orbit; it would be only a matter of time before it was "thrown off," unable to maintain its stable course around the nucleus. It would then spin out to a distant orbital shell, still cycling around the nucleus, but with less binding energy and at a slower pace. Suppose the electron had the wish to jump orbitals, back into the shell closer to the nucleus, a tremendous input of energy would be required to "jump it" back in.

Likewise it takes less energy input to cause fission, the splitting apart of an atom, than it does to cause fusion, the bringing together into unification. It takes far less energy to split apart than to exert the energy to work through situations and stay together.

And so it was with me. I had been in a tight orbital with Amma, but my negative tendencies had caused a dissonance on my path, and I hurled myself out to the hinterlands of the outer orbitals during the period from 1990-1996 where the nucleus exerts less effect on the errant electron. Although I had tried to jump back into my position in close orbit, coming back to the ashram for the years from 1993–96, ultimately my effort was misplaced. I was putting too many conditions on spiritual life, and not seeing that it was for me to surrender to what spiritual life wanted to show me, not the other way around.

Although I did manage a few more laps in an orbital closer to the nucleus, when the discordant vibration began again, it did not take much to dislodge me a second time to an outer orbital even further from the nucleus than the first time. At that distance, electrons can be stripped away from the original atom that they were part of, attracted by another nucleus that may be in proximity exerting a force of attraction to capture electrons into its own orbitals. For the electron to ever have a chance at rejoining its original location in the atomic structure is next to impossible; the energy required to 'jump' towards the nucleus is immeasurable. Let's just call that inordinate amount of energy, 'grace.'

Returning to Amma in the 1990's after my first departure, I placed my own set of conditions on the spiritual path – it should be thus and such a way, like it was in my former days, I should be with Amma whenever I wanted, based on my past proximity. But life doesn't work like that. When these desires were not fulfilled, when these conditions were not met, I caved in. I did make an effort to resume spiritual life, but it was not "right effort" to borrow a phrase from the Buddhists. I had tried to make the path fit to my limited concept of what it should be, instead of surrendering my ideas and letting the spiritual path remake me.

It's a bit like being overweight and going into a dress shop and having an idea about the look you want, but not fitting into anything because you haven't lost the weight.

Then leaving the dress shop in a huff because the clothes didn't fit. I justified to myself that I had made effort, but wouldn't admit to myself that it had not been the right kind.

If my first departure was in large part due to my lack of balance on the path because of the negative mindset I had gotten into, then when I left Amma the second time, it was because the spiritual path had not met my expectations. I was giving up on the path itself, and it felt like it was really for good. I had made a conscious choice to settle for less.

I lost sight of myself as a seeker; the love for the goal had dried up and spiritual life had become mechanical. Writing this today, these seem like small things that could have been easily reconciled. But I had left them to fester. This is our ego which causes such a major mishap on our spiritual path; first the fracturing of the Guru-disciple relationship, and then a breaking of the bond between the seeker and the path. The ego becomes aware of the possibility of its own sublimation and jumps in to save its skin! What started out initially as small things became huge obstacles because I underestimated them and was not careful to immediately address them. A slight drifting should be immediately corrected when treading the spiritual path. Amma often refers to the business man who tallies his account each night to see his profit or loss; spiritual seekers must do the same and not consider our day complete until we have done so. Otherwise, to continue on the path in the presence of the Guru, to remain in the orbital, will be very difficult. We must nurture our love for the goal at all cost and maintain a careful awareness (shraddha) of our daily progress on the path.

Some might ask, if Amma is all-knowing, all power-ful, why didn't she save you? But the beauty of Amma's way of teaching is that she doesn't force anything. Amma has repeatedly said, "When the flower is ready to open, it will open." You cannot pry open a rosebud to enjoy a beautiful, fragrant flower. One of the first qualities a seeker must have is patience. We only learn patience through a patient teacher, just as a nurturing mother raises her beloved child. In this way, Amma has the patience of the ocean and allows each seeker to progress at their chosen pace. It is one of the greatest testaments to Amma's teach-ing method.

So there I was, out on my own. From 1983 when I first came to Amma, through my second departure in 1996, my "career path" was spiritual seeking. Now, I had taken my eggs from that basket to place them in the basket of the world. Even then I knew that nothing could ever come close to what I had experienced with Amma in those 14 years, but maybe my problem was that I just had to learn to settle for less. If I lowered the bar of expectation, maybe I could eke out a bit of fleeting happiness from the world, instead of setting the bar so high that I was constantly falling short.

Having given spiritual life four more years of effort, I had been utterly defeated. I had tried and failed. Maybe someday I would be able to make sense of it all, but for the time being I tried not to be too hard on myself; there was no point in beating a dead horse. I would try to salvage some vestige of life in the West without doing myself in this time. I returned to New Mexico.

I decided to go back to school and settled on the idea of medicine. All my science course work from UC Berkeley was long outdated, so I began tackling a pre-med curriculum at the local community college, just to see if I still had the right stuff. In conjunction with that, I also enrolled in a paramedic course, as I would have to work to finance my way through school, and that seemed like an obvious interim career choice if I was going into medicine. I did well in every class and got licensed as an Emergency Medical Technician (EMT). I also became a teaching assistant for the life-sciences department at the University of New Mexico. In this way, two years passed.

MY GRANDMOTHER'S HOUSE

My grandmother had fallen ill in Pennsylvania, and I drove back during my summer break to take care of her. She was just turning 92 and was delightful to be around. She had recently been diagnosed with Alzheimer's, but was hardly affected by the disease. We got to talking about days-gone-by and that brought back a flood of memories of my difficult childhood. But it was alright now; I was healed of that trauma. By Amma.

Amma. The sweetness of that name. Why did spiritual life have to be so confusing! Yes, deep down inside I was missing her. I loved her still, so much that I cried for her that night, for the first time in a long time. I had shut Amma out, burned that bridge, was not a spiritual seeker anymore. Been there, done that. Just an average person, muddling along, along — a longing for a hug.

It was the Fourth of July weekend coming up and I realized that Amma would be somewhere nearby, maybe Chicago, or maybe even Washington DC. That was only a four-hour drive away! The next morning I wracked my brain, how could I find out Amma's tour schedule? By going to the grocery store and finding *Yoga Journal* in the magazine rack, of course! Since 1987, we would always buy one advertisement in *Yoga Journal* and, sure enough, there it was. The 1998 US Tour Schedule. And Amma's Washington DC program was being held over the Fourth of July weekend. What a coincidence.

WASHINGTON DC

Without giving any chance for my mind to resist, I arranged for my grandmother's care, packed a bag, and jumped in my truck to drive south. It was such a spontaneous thing to do, but my soul was stomping its feet to go see Amma, and my ego lost that round. Entering the hall was easier this time. I had already done this before. But I had to put aside a lot of shame and remorse — a small price to pay considering how royally I had acted.

No one seemed to notice me this time, not like when I had gone to see Amma in Berkeley, and it had been a gushing homecoming. No, this time it was very quiet. I got in the darshan line and took my turn like everyone else. As I got closer there was awareness that "Kusuma's here and going for Amma's darshan," since I could see familiar faces crowding in on the periphery. I kept my eyes on Amma until she looked into me. Amma smiled affectionately, her face beaming with love, and took me in her arms. "Kusumam, Kusumam, *ponnumol*, darling daughter, darling daughter…" There were tears again, on both sides, and Amma held me, swaying side to side, without letting go. A song came into my mind, and I softly sang the verse into Amma's ear:

Kannunir kondu nin padam kazhukam,
Katyayani ni kaivitalle…

With my tears, I will wash Your feet,
O Goddess Katyayani, but please do not forsake me…

Amma had me sit next to her for some time and we talked. She wanted to know how I was and what was I doing now. Yes, medical school, very good. Taking care of Grandma, yes, very good. There was not a trace of judgment on Amma's part, but the mood was different this time, and although Amma's energy felt the same, I had crossed a line with my second departure. For some time I sat in quiet contemplation, then Amma asked me to take my meal and turned her attention back to the darshan line.

The other person I was able to meet was Suneeti. Apparently she had taken formal initiation as she was wearing yellow robes! My heart felt so much joy watching her approach me from across the hall with some other friends in tow. She was radiant and peaceful, she was Brahmacharini Nirmalamrita. We walked together to the dining hall and I noticed she had lost a lot of weight. A memory from years gone by percolated up through my mind. Something about it left me with an uneasy feeling. When we had gotten our meals and found a quiet corner, we chatted a bit. I heartily congratulated her on taking formal initiation and added that it made me so happy to see how much she was loving her life and growing spiritually. Her eyes were bright and now that we were sitting down I could really feel how the peacefulness of her presence had grown.

She thought medical school was a great choice for me. New Mexico was a good place for me too; she knew it was my home now, but didn't say that. There was not a hint of judgment on her part either, she was genuinely glad to see me. I felt the opening and I inquired about her health. Yes, it was ok. She said she was tired, overseeing the retreat registrations was a big job. Being on tour was tiring, that's true. But she looked away when I asked if she had she been keeping up with her annual checkups, "Not really." I left it at that.

I knew that she had a lot of work to get through that night, so I said goodbye. There were volumes to share between us, but the moment was closing now. More old friends had spotted me and were coming over to say hi, so we shared a quick hug, a meaningful look and parted. Then my breath caught in my throat, and she was gone. I had seen something, what was it? Maybe it was nothing, just my imagination.

All the swamis made time to greet me and ask about my health, my plans, my family. The way they spoke was warm and sincere; their gentleness touched my heart. How much it must have hurt them to have me leave Amma a second time. After all the trials and tests we had gone through together, I think they were truly happy to see me and to know that I was alright. They were still my spiritual brothers and would not turn a cold shoulder to me or judge me harshly. That was apparent.

I took proper leave of Amma and drove back to Pennsylvania. I could not bear to see Devi Bhava for some reason. It was enough to digest just seeing Amma and meeting my former life again on such different terms.

TESTING, TESTING, ONE-TWO, ONE-TWO

I began to study in earnest for the MCAT exam. It would take about a year to be fully prepared. *One year* — I thought, there were a lot of things I had pulled off "in one year." But it wouldn't help me keep my focus if let my mind wander back in time. So I didn't. Latin, physiology, anatomy, chemistry, biology — my head was swimming.

THE MONTH OF MAY

This was a big month. First, I had final exams for the tail

end of my pre-med coursework and then the MCAT at month's end. If I did well, I could start applying to med schools by summer's end. I had started chanting my mantra again, actually since Washington DC, but especially lately. It gave me so much peace and concentration. Not that I felt I deserved it, but that was a different suitcase that needed unpacking. And then the phone rang.

It was Hari Sudha calling from Berkeley. Suneeti — Nirmalamrita — was back from India. But it was not good news. She had fallen ill, very ill and she wanted to see me. That's why Hari was calling. Could I come right away? I was trying to understand the urgency in the moment. I mean, I was in New Mexico and exams were starting next week, and then, and then… I knew. I knew why she was calling.

Yes, Hari, of course I would come. Please tell Suneeti I am getting off the phone and making arrangements to fly out. I hung up and sprang into action. This was it. She had made the deal we had spoken of years ago and she would die now. That was what I had seen last year, but couldn't put my finger on it. I threw clothes in my backpack and drove to campus to find my chemistry professor. I knew Suneeti, and I knew I didn't have much time.

Chemistry was my first exam; the professor was in his office. On seeing me he could tell that something was seriously wrong and stopped what he was doing.

"Yes, yes, come in. What is it Gretchen? What is it?"

I told him that I wouldn't be able to take the exam, as my best friend had been hospitalized in California.

"Oh, that sounds very serious. Yes, yes, of course you should go... Wait, just a minute, let me look up your marks. Hmmm, well, you're at the top of the class. Look, this sounds like something you really need to do. Consider yourself excused from the exam. Don't worry; your marks to date will be enough. I hope your friend is alright."

My knees felt weak as I walked to the parking lot. It was a two-hour drive to Albuquerque airport; my flight landed in Oakland early in the evening. Hari Sudha picked me up and told me what was going on — advanced cancer. She had just come back from India to the Bay Area for treatment; the doctor who had saved her life twice was on the case. But I knew that Nirmalamrita had blown off her annual checkup for who knows how many years. She had said as much last year in DC. I knew in my heart that she had known the cancer was back, and had picked the second choice.

When I came into the ICU room the next morning, Nirmalamrita was visibly ill, very ill, but radiating peace like I had never seen except in Amma. The cancer had spread everywhere. There was no way that a two-time cancer survivor as savvy as Nirmalamrita had not known the disease was spreading long ago. We looked into each other's eyes as I held her hand. She smiled so sweetly at me; we had not met for more than a year. She was calm and clear; her eyes were piercing mine with white pinpoints of light. Again, Amma's eyes. In a subdued tone I asked her if she had known. She shook her head in the affirmative. Did she cut the deal we had spoken of so many years before? Yes, she replied weakly, and squeezed my hand. No need to waste money, I want to be here with Amma when she comes, that was my plan...I interrupted and asked her to save her energy for seeing Amma in a few weeks. These things you are telling me, I already know.

Then she got right to the point. She asked me why I had left Amma. Was it my health? No, I told her, I had lost my nerve, I had stopped believing in myself. I had allowed my negativity to sweep me away. Would I ever go back? For good, not just for a visit? I was so choked up that I couldn't speak. She told me that would be one of her dying wishes.

The visiting hour had ended, it was time to go.

The next morning I went back to the hospital. No one was allowed into the ICU to see Nirmalamrita other than immediate family. Since I was tagged as "family," I was permitted access. Just as I was getting ready to enter into the sterile barrier to pass into the ward, I noticed one of Nirmalamrita's dearest friends, Sabari, also a cancer survivor, trying to get my attention. I went over to her and could see her distress. She was not being permitted in, but she wanted to say goodbye to Nirmalamrita; it was very important. Could I help her in any way? I thought for a moment and told her I would give her my time and got the nurses attention. In that way Sabari and Suneeti were able to meet one last time.

That night Nirmalamrita suffered a heart attack and fell into a coma. She emerged from her coma in time to receive a phone call from Amma and passed from this world less than a week later. When asked about Nirmalamrita's passing, Amma said that she had merged into Amma's heart and had attained God-realization.

Brahmacharini Nirmalamrita had gotten her time with Amma, not degraded by chemo, but serving as the coordinator for all of Amma's overseas spiritual retreats until a few weeks before passing away. She enjoyed 10 years of service living with Amma as a renunciate in India. Not bad odds for a person who suffered from cancer three times. She had known for years that it would be cancer that would come to take her from this world, but it was on her own terms, and she wouldn't have had it any other way.

Nirmalamrita's favorite Amma saying was the one about a spiritual aspirant needing to have the intensity for spiritual life that a person trapped in a burning house would have to escape. On the sidebar of her Sanskrit notebooks, during class, she would always draw flames; I would draw lotus flowers and dancing Goddesses. She was one of the rare individuals to have lived Amma's teaching to its fullest, and all who knew her are better for having kept her company.

JUNE BUG

Well, that was a mood changer. I got back to New Mexico and sat for my other exams, but felt lackluster about the MCAT. I could take it next month and not throw off my schedule too much; anyhow, I would need to get back into study mode, and that was not going to happen right at this moment. I did a lot of soul searching; Amma would be in Santa Fe in June, and I looked forward to seeing her.

Amma's program was held in the Santa Fe Wilderness Area, at a temple built for Amma by Steve and Amrita Priya Schmidt on their property. It could not have been a lovelier place to meet Amma again, with the fragrant pinon trees brushing up against the temple filled with memories, and the star-filled, New Mexico sky overhead. I came for the evening bhajan program; it was wonderful to hear Amma's singing again. After arati I went outside to look at the stars, and I felt my inspiration rising. I went around to the back of the temple and slipped onto the stage. Amma was seated down below, in front of the raised stage, giving darshan already. A dear friend, Swarna Iyer, was playing harmonium, and I caught her attention. I leaned forward and asked her permission to offer a song. I think she was surprised on two counts: I was the last person she expected to see, and I never sang. But she agreed and asked me which song. *Iswari Jagad Iswari.*

And so I sang to Amma, for the first time since I had sung the same song when she had left the Kalari to go roam around on a different starry night so many years ago.

When I sang the opening line, Amma turned around in her seat to look at me, but not with surprise. She already knew who it was singing:

Iswari jagadiswari paripalaki karunakari
Sasvata mukti dayaki mama khedamokke ozhikkanne...

O, Goddess, Goddess of the Universe,
O, Preserver, Giver of grace and eternal liberation
Please rid me of all my sorrow...

I went for Amma's darshan; it was very calm the feeling between us now; a powerful tranquility enveloped me. Something had adjusted. I don't know what, but that didn't matter. I sat near Amma for a long time and enjoyed the mood of devotion. Then it was time to go and I headed back, into the dark, starry night.

THE DOLDRUMS

The summer window for MCAT testing came and went. I was in the doldrums and questioned what I was doing. The beauty of Nirmalamrita's relationship with Amma was dazzling to me. How many people had come to Amma and made so much of their time? How had I let go so completely when my life with Amma had always held so much promise? Amma was a God-realized Master; in that I had no doubt. It was self-doubt which had swallowed me up. It wasn't that I didn't believe in the spiritual path or in Amma. I lacked the conviction when I was trying to practice while living in Amma's presence. I had just given up.

Having made that choice, how would I find peace living in the world, that was the question I kept turning over and over in my mind. Having spent more than two years in the planning stage to attend medical school, was that finally the right choice? Because if not, it would be better to decide that sooner rather than later.

Thumbing through the Yellow Pages phone book one afternoon, an advertisement caught my eye. "Earn Your Masters Degree at St. John's College-Santa Fe." In Eastern Classics. Hmmm, that's interesting. So, I called to find out more. It was a one-year intensive program. The language component was either Chinese or Sanskrit, and the bulk of the coursework was the study of the original scriptures of Hinduism and Buddhism and Taoism. I drove down for an interview and was accepted into the program. The course started in one week. It felt like an honest choice, to take time to sit with the great books of the East and think things over for a year. How could that not be helpful at this juncture?

One thing leads to another. I had to satisfy my nagging doubt about what to do with my life now that I had left Amma. So I had set out in one direction — medical school, and then got cold feet and went off in a more familiar direction, spirituality. What was wrong with me? Why couldn't I just be satisfied with what life offered and leave it at that? Why such a restless spirit?

One thing leads to another. In the process of getting my master's degree, I met my husband. We both thought having children was what we wanted. I got pregnant on our wedding night. While our baby girl was being born, I played "Ananta Srishti Vahini" on the CD player in the background. When we washed her head for the first time with the nurse in the hospital, I chanted Vedic mantras. Without telling each other, my husband and I each picked a name for the baby. We both picked "Mirabai." My husband was not into my spiritual quirkiness, but went along with it. *Maybe that will change*, I thought to myself. I brought Mirabai to Amma for her blessing.

What could Amma say? She always loves us no matter what. But it was difficult to walk through the door with such a clearly different choice having been made. I had gone off on my own and done what I wanted, and that was more a statement of who I was than anything Amma had done. I was a devotee now, a noble relationship, one more suited for me perhaps, loving Amma from a distance. But why wasn't my soul satisfied, why couldn't I just relax and enjoy the ride life had offered me?

2007 – NEVER TOO LATE

Everything happened so quickly that year. My mom had been diagnosed with cancer the previous year and was struggling through treatment. My father was diagnosed with cancer in April and died suddenly in Boston a few weeks later, before I got to see him and say goodbye. My 19-year Saturn period ended. My marriage was falling apart. And I came back to Amritapuri. With my daughter.

Ostensibly to have Amma bless my father's ashes, but to be honest, I had had enough.

I finally saw the light. It was so simple really, but I had spent years missing the point. Amma was here in our midst, and my restless soul was longing for the spiritual journey she offered. Love for love's sake, devotion because it was the highest emotion, the one that broke all my self-imposed barriers. I was finally mature enough to see that it was I who had set myself apart, and it was I who could set myself free. And that it was never too late to come back and try again.

This time I came back for the joy of it. I came back for the sweetness of love, the divine love, that I had never found anywhere in the world, in all my wandering. All those years standing apart from Amma in a world that held only an empty promise — only inevitable death and delusion, material gain and loss, selfishness and desire. I came back for the deeper, truer meaning that spiritual life offers. I came back to fulfill a dying sister's wish. I came back to prove to myself that I had the courage to face what I knew had to be done to make things right again. To stand before Amma and the community and tell them of my journey into darkness and of finding my way back. And to raise my daughter in Amma's magnificent presence, knowing that it is the greatest gift a mother could give her child. All my petty differences were of no consequence; it was my time to enjoy Amma's presence and serve as best I could. Without the angst, without the expectation of attaining anything. Just for the sheer joy of being in God's presence and bearing witness to it. To be here with my beautiful, inspiring community and serve with my whole heart. Amma put the smile back on my face. It is never too late.

Continuing the Journey

At the time of this writing, it has been five years since I have been back living in Amma's Amritapuri Ashram with my daughter Mirabai. Five glorious years that rival and surpass the indescribable sweetness of my early years with Amma.

Because I have had to work through an extremely difficult process, the victory of return is all the sweeter for that effort. Sometimes we must endure tremendous difficulty on the spiritual path, and in my case it was that very progression that has brought me to the profound joy I experience today. How can I regret this journey? Would I do some things differently given the chance? Of course. But the regrettable thing would be if I had never come back to Amma! It is not the falling down that is remarkable; it is the getting back up and moving forward that matters.

I have learned to see all situations as Amma's prasad (blessed offering) and to not react to or reject the hard times which, when digested properly, only serve to propel me forward spiritually. Amma always reminds us that there are no failures in our lives; they are all stepping stones to the final victory.

I am more mature and grounded now in my spiritual life, having made it through the darkness. I can now see how my early years with Amma established a solid foundation on which I could finally build a spiritual life that will see me through to the end. To learn to believe in myself was essential – that was what was lacking in my early efforts on the spiritual path. Because I know now, without a shadow of a doubt, that serving God in others is what I want to be doing with my life. Having my daughter by my side is integral to that. Who I was then as a renunciate in my twenties is not disconnected from who I am now as a mother. After all, Amma says that it is not external *sannyasa* (renunciation) that is important, but internal sannyasa — overcoming our likes and dislikes, putting others before ourselves, and living with the understanding that everything we consider our own is a temporary gift from God that will one day leave us.

My life today is the continuation of the journey that started in a bookstore in Copenhagen more than three decades ago. I am still pursuing the Divine Mother in the realm of my heart, and serving her in the living form we call "Amma." I serve her in order to make the world a better place; this is true service to the Guru. We never know what life will bring our way; good or bad, we don't get to choose. In the early years with Amma, I never imagined all these obstacles would stand in my way. But Amma is teaching us that it is how we choose to react toward our difficulties that makes all the difference.

Traveling the world on hope and a prayer, doing whatever I could in order to bring Amma to her children, I was able to overcome many trials and tribulations. However, in the face of the inner foes of my own negativity, I was not able to prevail so easily. Both circumstances presented challenges, one external, one internal. I had to find the right approach to surmount them both in order to learn what I needed to work through in this lifetime with Amma. In the scriptures it is said there are three kinds of disciples—those who can learn by being told, those who can learn by observing others' experiences, and those who learn through personal experience. Clearly, I belong to the third group!

I have experienced the truth that Amma is always with me, no matter what, and that she never gives up on her children. I have learned on every level that it is truly never too late. I am living spiritual life in Amma's divine presence again, happier than I ever was, side by side with my daughter; Amma is guiding us both, and showing me that there is no obstacle great enough to stop the ever-victorious Divine Mother.

I would like to share one last story: When Mirabai came to Amritapuri for the first time, she was five years old. She became aware that people were getting mantras and she wanted to know what that was. So I explained the basic idea of chanting a mantra and how it can bring us peace and wisdom if we chant it carefully. She wanted to know more about the idea of *ishta devata*, (the beloved deity) aspect of getting a mantra. Remember, she's five! So I went through the different deities: the Divine Mother, the Divine Mother as Amma, Lord Krishna, Kali Mata, Buddha, Jesus Christ, Lord Shiva... When I got to Shiva she wanted to know if he was the god who wears the animal skins. I said yes, and added that he rides on the bull Nandi in the Himalayas as well. She shook her head appreciatively and said, "That's the one I want!" Wow, I thought to myself, here is someone who knows what she wants! Is it by chance that she is my child and came to Amma so early in her life to grow up with Amma because of my own strong desire to finally return to Amritapuri?

The next day we went for darshan and she asked Amma, "Mantra, please!" and Amma nodded her head in agreement while looking intently at her. Then Mirabai leaned in as if to confide in Amma, and I heard her say, "Shiva mantra," just to make sure Amma knew which one to give her! Well, Amma found that hilarious and was commenting to all around her about what Mirabai had said. We stayed up to the end of the program and Mira was able to have mantra diksha that very night. I felt so blessed to be her mom. It seemed that she was going to get an early start on her spiritual journey with the best Guru the world has to offer.

One year later, when Mirabai was six, we were waiting in the darshan queue and I noticed she was writing a note to give to Amma. At one point she whispered to me, "Mom, how do you spell Amrita Vidyalayam?" I spelled it out for her and I was very curious to know what little Mira had in mind. When it was our turn for darshan, she gave her note to Amma, and the brahmacharini standing by Amma's side translated it.

Amma got a huge smile on her face and said in English, "Yes, Yes! Good! Good!" On her own initiative, Mira had asked Amma if she could attend Amma's school here in India. And so off we went. Checkered pinafore, bobby socks and all! At first it was really hard to adjust, but she did not give up. Mira is now in her fourth year at Amma's Amrita Vidyalayam School and is doing very well, in spite of all the homework in no less than three languages – Malayalam, Hindi and Sanskrit! Whenever there is a complaint about not wanting to go to school, I ask her to go to Amma and express herself since they had decided together on this plan.

To be on this path of love with my daughter Mirabai is a blessing beyond anything I ever imagined motherhood to be. She is growing strong, sure of herself, and constantly keeps me on my toes! She teaches me things that I had struggled to learn from Amma such as: patience, forbearance, empathy, selfless service, unconditional love, giving without expectation, not being attached to the fruit of our labor, maintaining an unwavering mind – all these qualities are brought out on a daily basis through motherhood. It's not that Amma wasn't teaching me those things; she constantly modeled these qualities for me, but I resisted learning. To survive motherhood with a spirited child one has no choice but to develop these qualities! Amma is brilliant at being Mother to the world.

What better place than Amritapuri to raise a child with spiritual values? The friends she has made in Amma's ashram will be friends for life. They play tag around the banyan tree at the front of the Kali Temple whenever they get the chance, and hide-and-go-seek until it is time to come running and sit near Amma for bhajans.

At last I can make out a deep harmony underlying all the twists and turns of my journey. It took me this many years to work through lessons someone else might have learned in a day. But this is how my story unfolded, however flawed it may seem. I have learned not to judge. What matters most is that when I hold Amma's hand, she shows me that I am the maker of my own destiny. However far I am ready to go, that far Amma will take me. Without fail.

Yes, I was blessed to be the instrument to bring Amma to the world. Yes, I was blessed to be here in the early days for an intensive spiritual training with Amma. But having lived here then and now, I can state without any hesitation that the same intensity that existed then, is still here now for the taking. Our relationship with Amma is what we make of it, which remains the same as on the day I met her. We are the limiting factor. It is what we bring to the journey that determines how quickly we reach the goal.

AMRITAPURI TODAY

With more people than ever in the ashram it does not mean that there is less opportunity for Self-realization, or that there is less spirituality here than there was in the early days. Amma is an enlightened Master and this is her ashram; her grace is flowing as vibrantly as it always has. It is for us to open our hearts to Amma. And when we do, Amma comes running. Amma is here in the same infinite capacity she has always been, spending hours and hours of her day keeping company with us, guiding thousands and thousands of people on the spiritual path with effortless ease, as fresh and full of laughter at the end of the night as when she arrived. She is constantly in our midst, arriving by mid-morning in the darshan hall, and many times not going back to her room until the wee hours of the morning of the next day. Then returning a few hours later for the next day's program and repeating it all again.

Amma fully participates in every aspect of ashram life, enthusiastically leading us in meditation, satsang, archana, bhajans and selfless service. There is not a single day in all these years when I have known Amma to take a day for herself. There is no other spiritual Master who makes themselves more available or gives more of their own personal time and energy than Amma does. She makes everything fun and full of sweetness when it comes to spiritual life. Amma's entire life is lived out in the open, and anyone who wants to interact personally with Amma can do so.

Is there another person on the planet who gives more of herself for the good of the world? Amma lives in the same small room she did the day I met her. It is in the most central, noisiest part of the ashram, where the smokestack from the ashram kitchen vents out, where there is no view from the window. But Amma refuses any resources to be directed for her comfort. She takes nothing for herself, except for the troubles of the world upon her shoulders, all the while giving peace and succor to those who come for her blessing.

EMBRACING THE WORLD

While I was busy sorting myself out, Amma was also busy. What started as a handful, then a dozen, then the first hundred, has led to tens of thousands, and now more than 32 million people have experienced Amma's divine embrace. There is not a single person who has met and spent time with Amma who does not have a special story to share. There is the "before I met Amma" part and the "after I met Amma" part of our lives. Our lives have become imbued with the fragrance of peace, contentment and kindness because of our contact with Amma's sheltering arms. It all starts there, resting our head on her strong shoulder. Without asking anything from us, Amma has given us the treasure that is greater than gold — the chance to selflessly serve others as an expression of our love for God in a world that is desperate need of love. This perfect Master and great humanitarian has inspired millions to do good for others in more than 60 countries around the world.

In just 25 years, Amma has established a vast network of worldwide charities, all aimed at meeting basic human

needs wherever and whenever possible. Building houses
for the homeless, providing scholarships for school-age
children and vocational training for women in rural areas,
conducting medical camps in some of the most remote
corners of India, responding immediately to alleviate the
suffering of the victims when natural disasters strike, improv-
ing quality of life for the world's poor by providing clean
drinking water, and protecting the future with value-based
youth groups, environmental initiatives and a wide array
of research projects with a humanitarian orientation. Her
devotees named this charitable network "Embracing the
World," in recognition of the fact that Amma's selfless act
of embracing each person who comes to her — as many
hours of every day of her life as it takes — is the engine
that powers this broad-based humanitarian movement
sowing seeds of compassion throughout the world.

Since 1987, Amma has traveled to six of the world's
seven continents, and 26 countries worldwide have hosted
Amma's programs including Australia, Austria, Belgium,
Brazil, Canada, Chile, Finland, France, Germany, Ireland,
Italy, Japan, Kenya, Kuwait, Malaysia, Mauritius, the
Netherlands, Russia, Singapore, Spain, Sri Lanka, Swe-
den, Switzerland, the United Arab Emirates, the United
Kingdom and the United States of America. The French
territory of Reunion Island has also graciously hosted
Amma's programs for more than 25 years.

In addition, there are 38 countries where Amma has
sent her disciples to lead programs, but has yet to visit;

or where there are Amma Centers, activities or service projects going on in her name:

Bulgaria, Czech Republic, Denmark, Estonia, Greece, Hungary, Luxembourg, Norway, Poland, Portugal, Slovenia and Turkey in Europe; Argentina, Colombia, Costa Rica, Haiti, Mexico, Peru and Venezuela in South & Central America; China, Hong Kong, Indonesia, the Philippines, Taiwan and Thailand in Asia; Bahrain, Egypt, Israel, Jordan, Lebanon, Oman, and Qatar in the Middle East; Fiji, Guam, Papua New Guinea and New Zealand in Oceania; and Botswana & South Africa in Africa.

In the annals of history, there is no mention of a person who has lived as Amma has lived, literally embracing the world, her active compassion and all-encompassing wisdom pouring out like a torrent of pure grace. Generations from now, people will read about Amma and be reminded of true sacrifice and genuine selfless service.

When I stop and reflect on how expansive Amma's humanitarian and spiritual endeavor has become since I left America to come in search of the Divine Mother 29 years ago, I am humbled to have been able to play a small part in the development of her mission. I also wonder if we are not rather closer to the beginning than the end of this story.

Glossary

Arati—the ceremonial waving of burning camphor before the deity; symbolizes self-surrender to God or Guru, just as the camphor burns away without a trace, so too does the ego

Archana – refers to the chanting aloud or internally of the 108 or 1000 names of a particular deity (e.g. the Lalita Sahasranama)

Ashram – a spiritual center where a community of spiritual seekers live

Avatar – a divine incarnation of God in human form

Bhajan – the practice of devotional singing, or can refer to a devotional song

Brahmacharin(i) – Male (or female) renunciate who lives a life of service to God, celibacy and control of the senses

Brahman – The ultimate Truth beyond any attributes; the omniscient, omnipotent, omnipresent substratum of the universe.

Brahmasthanam Temple – the unique temple(s) consecrated by Amma with a four-sided deity facing in the four directions to symbolize Unity in diversity. One face of the deity is Ganesha, the elephant God who is the remover of obstacles, one face of the deity is the Divine Mother, one face is Lord Shiva represented by the Shiva Lingham, a formless representation of Shiva, and the fourth side is Rahu, a malevolent planet that can be propitiated through specific worship to ward off malefic influences in a person's life.

Bhasmam – sacred ash, also referred to as vibhuti

Chakras – energy centers in the body

Darshan – literally means 'view, sight', but in the context of this book it refers to meeting a holy person and receiving their blessing

Devi Bhava Darshan – the Mood of the Divine Mother, refers to the time when Amma sits in the temple wearing the beautiful dress and crown of the Divine Mother to bless the devotees who come for her darshan, a time when Amma reveals her oneness with the Divine Mother aspect in a more obvious way

Diksha – initiation

Hari Katha – the story of the Lord, refers to a musical narrative of the life of a saint, a sage, or a God or Goddess

Ishta Devata – literally, Beloved Deity; how one refers to the object of one's meditation on the aspect of God with form

Japa – repetition of a mantra, many times in sets of 108

Kindi – ceremonial brass pot used for holding water during the worship

Kirtan – devotional singing

Kumkum – the red powder put on the third eye of the middle point of the forehead, especially favored by the Divine Mother aspect of God

Mahatma – literally, Great Soul; refers to one who abides in the state of Oneness with the Universal Self

Manasa puja – performing ritualistic worship mentally

Mantra – sacred formula, a set of words or syllables chanted in Sanskrit to purify the atmosphere and the practitioner's mind

Mantra diksha – initiation into the use of a mantra; it is considered a tremendous blessing to receive mantra diksha from a Realized Soul who imparts their blessing and a part of their awakened consciousness at the time of initiation

Mantra shakti – the power invested in a mantra, especially one conferred by a Realized Soul like Amma

Maya – Universal Illusion, Power of Brahman

Murti – statue of a deity

Mridangam – two-faced drum

Pada puja – ceremonial washing of the Guru's feet as an expression of love and respect, and acknowledging the Supreme Truth that the Guru's feet represent

Peetham – seat offered for the deity to sit on, generally refers to the chair on which Amma sits, especially during the Devi Bhava Darshan

Pranam – prostration or show of respect through bowing before the deity or the Guru

Prasad – a blessed offering or gift from a holy person or temple, often in the form of food.

Prema – Supreme Love, Divine Love, or unconditional love

Rajasic – the active aspect of the three qualities: tamasic, rajasic, sattvic

Sadhana – spiritual practices which purify the practitioner, such as meditation, mantra japa, study of the scriptures, yoga, satsang, selfless service, etc.

Samadhi – literally, "cessation of all mental vacillations," a transcendental state in which the individual self is united with the Supreme Self

Sankalpa – divine resolve or intention, when referring to Amma, it often signifies that she is giving her blessing for a beneficial outcome

Sannyasa – formal vows of renunciation after which one wears ochre-colored robes to represent the burning away of all desires.

Satsang – being in communion with the Supreme Truth. Also being in the company of a Mahatma, listening to a spiritual talk or discussion, participating in spiritual practices in a community of spiritual seekers.

Sattvic – quality of purity, light and spiritual subtleness, one of the three qualities: tamasic, rajasic, and sattvic

Seva – selfless service, the results of which are dedicated to God

Shraddha – awareness, faith

Talam – the beat or the count of a song

Tamasic – quality of darkness, inertia, laziness; one of the three qualities: tamasic, rajasic, sattvic

Tirtham – holy water, also refers to a body of water near a holy place or temple such as a pond or pool of water for bathing before entering the temple

Vasana – latent tendencies, or subtle desires within the mind which manifest as action and habits